Ena Mirren was born in London ~~~~ dren, but in 1970 her eldest son ~~~~ traffic accident. Following his de~~~~ then went on to train as a social worker at Southampton University. She worked for Wiltshire County Council practising generic social work, which covered child care, mental health and the needs of the elderly. She specialised in mental health until her retirement in January 1994.

She was on the national committee of The Compassionate Friends from 1979 to 1992 and now supervises Cruse counsellors. She has lived in the Salisbury area for the last nineteen years.

The Compassionate Friends (TCF) was founded in Coventry in 1969 when the Revd. Simon Stephens witnessed two sets of bereaved parents helping each other and realised the therapeutic value of their friendship. He realised that such support and guidance could be helpful to bereaved parents everywhere.

He arranged the first meeting of bereaved parents in the area and from this local support groups were set up throughout the country. TCF is now a national and international organisation.

OUR CHILDREN

Coming to terms with the loss of a child:
Parents' own stories

Ena Mirren
with
The Compassionate Friends

Hodder & Stoughton

First published in Great Britain in 1995 by Hodder and Stoughton Ltd.
A division of Hodder Headline PLC

10 9 8 7 6 5 4 3 2 1

British Library Cataloguing in Publication Data

Mirren, Ena
  Our Children: Coming to Terms with the
  Loss of a Child
  I. Title
  306.88

ISBN 0340 62863 4

Typeset by Phoenix Photosetting, Chatham, Kent
Printed and bound in Great Britain by
Mackays of Chatham PLC, Chatham, Kent

Hodder and Stoughton
A division of Hodder Headline PLC
338 Euston Road
London NW1 3BH

This book is dedicated to the memory of my beloved son, Michael, 17.11.51–20.11.70, whose untimely death took me to the depths of despair, although the memories of his life gave me the courage to use my pain to help others and in so doing help myself.

It is also dedicated to the memories of the children whose stories are written within its pages. I know the pain, joy and tears that have been shed in the writing, and the pride with which their stories have been written.

Last, but not least, to those whose stories are not included here, whose experiences nonetheless run through the threads of those stories that have.

ACKNOWLEDGMENTS

I would like to thank Marilyn McGowan, a friend and school counsellor, for helping me to get my thoughts into some sort of order that would be comprehensible to readers. Also Jan Johnson Newell for her tireless energy in typing and retyping manuscripts, Jill Sherratt for using her lunch-hours to type endless letters to publishers and writers. My thanks also go to my new husband, Tony, for his forbearance in the project, which did not involve him but which he knows means a lot to me, and my children, Jackie, Sheila and Alan, who have put up with me as a mother with all my human faults and frailties.

CONTENTS

INTRODUCTION

Mourning has a quite precise physical task to perform. Its function is to detach the survivor's memories and hopes from the dead.[1]

In November 1970 my nineteen-year-old son, Michael, was killed in a road traffic accident. This was every parent's nightmare come true. I was plunged into an unreal world of pain, despair, disbelief – the world of loss and grief. The mourning was to come later. I was surrounded by people who did not know how to help. I felt helpless and alone. My husband buried himself in his work.

There is a great need for this book. A lot of books on grief have been written from a very personal perspective, recounting survival through faith or the experience of a particular illness or death. Other books written from a theoretical perspective have emphasised the process of mourning rather than the personal experience of grief. But this book is different. It is written by people who have lost children and therefore expresses a grief that is unique to the individual parent, but which, at the same time, covers all types of loss – accident, illness, drowning, suicide, murder – and all aspects of the grieving process – the feelings of shock, denial, disbelief, anger, guilt, sadness, depression, insomnia, loss of appetite and, finally, acceptance.

The pain of grief can be measured by the depth and intensity of a relationship and it is doubtful if there is any deeper bond than that between a parent and child. Each of these accounts represents a personal disaster, but also serves to express ways in which parents have overcome their loss. The loss of a child means the loss of the future. All parents live through their children. Although we may not care to accept this, it is undeniable when death comes – the future of the child is gone and, with it, part of theirs: the Mothering Sunday card that never comes, the birthdays that are never celebrated, the Christmases with the empty chair, the loss of potential grandchildren and the loss of support, love and care as you get older, seeing them grow up, letting them go to live their own life. This is made all the more painful by comparison with their friends – seeing them go through the stages of living, celebrating their birthdays, their weddings, the birth of their children. Parents bereaved of their child experience the loss of their life as they know it and feel that for others life goes on, whereas for them it has ended.

Life afterwards can never be the same. An emotional blunting takes place and the ability to show love and care can become very difficult. Fear of further loss can affect relationships. Women in particular may not be able to have a sexual relationship – how can you enjoy yourself when your child is dead? It could be that they are denying the act that brought the child into being. On the other hand, fears for other children may make parents over-protective. Fears are heightened in grief: a telephone call late at night, early in the morning, a policeman at the door, are all triggers that can set the mind racing with fear.

The first feelings after the death, whether it was expected or as the result of an accident, murder or suicide, are shock, disbelief, denial. It isn't true; he *will* walk in shortly; she *will* get better. The numbness that follows shock can cushion the bereaved temporarily. I was told at 11.30 p.m. that my son was dead. I was visiting my sister in London at the time. My brother-in-law drove us through the night back to Salisbury. Holding my sleeping four-year-old son in my arms, I looked up at the clear starlit night – which star was he? Was he looking down on me? It wasn't true. If I could get home I could save him; after all, I was his mother.

The denial and disbelief can linger. It is not the same for everybody. One young mum I met was still in a state of denial three months on, living a fairly normal life and wondering why those around her were mourning.

For five days I felt sure it had been a mistake. My son would come home. Not until I saw him in his coffin did I accept that he was dead.

Guilt is a component of grief. Guilt at not protecting a child from whatever was the cause of death. Irrational maybe, but very real. Guilt at the times one had grumbled or chastised, or refused them things. It is not until later that the memories of the good times come back. Most parents feel guilt at still being alive, feeling, Why not us? Why the child who has his life before him? The 'if onlys' – words well known to bereaved parents. If only I hadn't let him have a bike/car; if only I had called the doctor/ambulance, sooner. If only I had been there to say 'mind how you go', my son would not have been killed. Later, when you are rational, you know that is not true, but at that time the irrational thoughts take over.

Parents in grief will experience all sorts of strange thoughts and feelings. Grief leaves people irrational, feeling mad, out of focus, totally detached from life as they know it. They may be suicidal, wanting to join their dead child. They may think they see the child in the street, in the house, or in another child. One mother of a six-year-old boy killed by a car had to take her other children to the same school. She developed a fixation on another child who looked like her dead son and found herself watching for him each day. Luckily she was able to contain these feelings through counselling sessions so that she did not frighten the boy or his mother.

One landmark that can again cause a recurrence of irrational fears in the death of an older child is when they have been dead longer than they have lived. Michael was nineteen years and three days old when he was killed. I had some very sad feelings when his thirty-eighth birthday came around. Also, at the time when his brother reached his nineteenth birthday, there was anxiety about whether he would make it or not. There is no rationale in grief.

Parents of a dead child of whatever age may read the death columns in the newspapers and feel angry when expressions of loss are made for someone really old – they've had their life; my child did not. Losses after the death of a child can bring mixed reactions. I could not go to a funeral for at least two years. It brought back too many painful memories.

Anger is a strong emotion sometimes projected towards doctors or nurses for not saving the child, or towards the person or persons responsible for the death, towards the spouse or whoever was looking after the child. One can feel anger towards the child for dying, particularly in cases of suicide, but often in other cases too. Why did he go out in that car? Why did he go out with that person? Why did he put himself in the position where this could happen to him? Why did he have to die when I needed him? Anger towards God who could allow this to happen is also common. Faith can be strengthened or tested and fail. I was very angry towards God, whom I trusted, but who allowed my son to be killed. I then felt guilt at being angry with God.

One of the longest, and often loneliest, stages of grief is the third stage – sadness, despair, depression. The support systems that were around in the immediate aftermath of the loss have gone; others' lives go on and they move forward. For the bereaved, time often stands still. The pain of grief is with them; it can affect their physical and mental well-being. It may require some medical input. Weight loss, insomnia, all kinds of illness and susceptibility to virus are sometimes part of this stage. One can flit to and fro in these stages. If an inquest is to be held, this becomes a landmark. If the result is not what is expected, or wanted, this can renew feelings of guilt, anger and pain. If one has a bad day after good days, the bad day appears to be worse. If one laughs, or forgets the dead child for a short period, one feels guilty again.

Acceptance is the final stage of grief. Bereaved parents will get quite angry if someone says 'I'm glad to see you've got over it.' One learns to live with the loss and internalise the dead child – the good memories come back and can be enjoyed.

There is no time limit on any of these stages, nor on the process of grief. It does not depend only on the depth of love one has for the dead child, but on lots of other factors – the personality of the bereaved, how many previous losses one has had and how they have been coped with, what support systems one has and the accessibility of self-help groups, whether the parents are able to grieve together, or unable to share their pain. As acceptance comes, a change in direction and attitude to life comes too. People change jobs, move, take up new hobbies. Campaigning for a cause close to the heart may have been a coping strategy, but this need may now have been spent or have settled down to a less intense state. There is sometimes guilt at this stage as one feels disloyal to the dead child for not continuing to mourn, but the bereaved parent can also accept that, by living, one is doing what the child would have wanted one to do.

Years later a piece of music, a smell or something in a book may trigger a memory. Close friends of mine whose son was killed found certain music sent them into floods of tears. For me Simon and Garfunkel's 'Bridge over Troubled Water', the last record Michael bought, brings me comfort and brings Michael closer to me for a short while.

My son has now been dead for twenty-four years. He is still a part of my life, but not that of my present husband, who was not his father. Few of my present friends knew him; those that did and have good memories I cherish. I have accepted his death – there is no alternative – but I cannot help wondering how different life would be if he were alive now. I feel sure I will meet him again one day. I am not afraid to die, but feel I still have a lot of living to do first.

Every parent who has lost a child, of whatever age, through whatever circumstance, will find something in *Our Children* they can relate to. This book will not have all the answers. It will not *tell you* how long you should grieve for, it will not *tell you* what you should do with your child's belongings, nor will it *tell you* how to work through your grief or when to stop grieving. What it aims to do is to help and guide you through your own grief by relating the experiences of other bereaved parents. Above all, it will make you realise you are not alone in your feelings.

It will also be useful to those who know people who have lost a child and those in the caring professions who help people to cope with loss. As well as learning from the stories what helps bereaved parents, there is a special advice and information section at the back of the book.

The contributors are mainly women, but the bereaved fathers have been very involved in the telling of the stories and, as the reader will see, their thoughts and feelings run through the book. We unfortunately live in a society where men aren't supposed to cry, which means that men are not allowed to express their pain and grief openly. I hope that by reading these stories many bereaved fathers will find help and comfort in handling their grief.

As one reads through the stories so the threads of the grieving process can be seen. The familiar thoughts and feelings run through no matter how different the loss or whatever the age or social group. The death of a child is the greatest leveller of people. The pain of losing a child knows no boundaries. The bond between bereaved parents is timeless. To quote one story, 'We do not sit and be miserable when we are together. We can have our tears because we are with others who understand; we can share our memories and not feel we are imposing.'

I have shared these stories with the writers during the process of editing. Although I may not have met them, I feel I now know these children and their families well. I feel privileged to have done so.

Ena Mirren
September 1994

FOREWORD BY
COUNTESS MOUNTBATTEN
OF BURMA

Nicky

He took his big candle
And went into another room
I cannot find
But I know he was here
Because of all the happiness
He left behind [2]

As Patron of The Compassionate Friends I am pleased to have been asked to contribute to this collection of personal experiences because I believe very strongly that talking, reading, or writing about traumatic personal tragedies can be the greatest help in coming to terms with them.

Our own first, small, but very real tragedy was the birth of a still-born son (our third child) in the days when no help of any sort was given, or deemed necessary, to help cope with the grief involved. It was a difficult and lonely business finding our way back to the world.

Our real family tragedy dates back to August 1979, so time has exerted its healing powers as far as possible where once we almost doubted that it could ever do so. But, of course, if our lives have not been exactly ruined completely, they will most certainly never be the same again.

We were very proud parents of seven children (three boys, two girls and identical twin boys) with seventeen years between eldest and youngest. Every summer for over thirty years the whole family, as far as possible, together with my sister and her three children, would join our father at his small 'castle' in the west of Ireland for a month's precious family holiday. Then, in 1979, the IRA placed a bomb in my father's small thirty-foot fishing boat. They watched from the shore while two old people, three children, a woman and one middle-aged man got in and sailed off on a peaceful fishing expedition on a glorious day and then deliberately detonated the bomb by remote control. Of the seven people in the boat, four were killed – my father (seventy-nine), mother-in-law (eighty-three), elder twin son, Nicholas (fourteen) and the local boy, Paul (fifteen), who ran the boat. My husband, the other twin, Timothy, and I were so badly injured we nearly died, and it was about a year before we could return to a more or less normal life.

The intensity of the pain caused by the death of our twin, a particularly caring and loving child, dwarfed the pain of the loss of our parents for my husband and me; so much so that I began to feel almost guilty that I could not mourn the death of my father properly, because he and I were particularly close.

We were greatly helped through the early stages of our intense pain by being blessed with a very close and loving family with whom we spent endless hours just talking of our losses. Looking back now I realise that suffering pain makes one self-centred, and I wonder whether we were aware enough how much the other 'children' were suffering over the death of their beloved brother. I think children are often unintentionally overlooked in their own very real grief.

Certainly, I was very aware of the deep and cruel trauma Timothy must be suffering at the loss of the other half of himself, and this worried me greatly. I know the greatest help he found, both then and later, was being able to talk to another bereaved twin and not needing to explain what he felt. I became aware that both consciously and unconsciously Timmy was taking on some of Nicky's characteristics because he felt that now he 'had to do everything for both of us'.

We were also greatly helped by the hundreds of letters and messages, not only from friends, but often from total strangers who had heard of the tragedy, and this was a real source of support. I have learned always to write to a bereaved friend or acquaintance (and occasionally even to a stranger), no matter how late the letter may be. Indeed, I found often that the letters that arrived weeks, or even months, later were especially appreciated because they meant that people were still remembering us.

In our case, the letters I truly valued were the few from people who understood that, to us, the real tragedy was the loss of Nicky, although most people seemed to think, understandably, more about my father's death. The only really unhelpful ones encouraged one 'to try and forget the tragedy' – as if we ever could, or would want to.

It was also sad when people tried to avoid any mention of those who had been killed, thinking that this would be upsetting, when we desperately wanted to talk about them and keep their memory fresh and alive. The only faintly amusing aspect was the highly embarrassed discomfort of anyone who talked by mistake of Nicky instead of Timmy. I still try to reassure people that actually hearing Nicky's name spoken reinforces the belief that he is still part of our family.

Mercifully, neither my husband nor I feel bitter about our loss, as this can be such an all-pervading, corroding influence on the lives of all around one as well as on one's own life. This does not mean that we do not feel the deepest eternal sorrow at our loss – even now tears are never buried so deep that they do not reappear unexpectedly.

Having learned to come to terms with our grief, which seemed to take about two years, makes it very much easier to help other people to cope with their own grief because, however unfortunately, you share a common bond in your loss and have no difficulty in expressing your sympathy and understanding of what a bereaved person is enduring. We found this shared grieving to be particularly valuable when the five-year-old daughter (third child) of our eldest son and daughter-in-law died after a very brave year's battle with a kidney tumour and much suffering. As a grandparent, to see your own child overcome with grief, and to be unable to do much to help, is an extra dimension to sorrow.

I think the lesson I have learned from grief is principally to get your priorities right and to differentiate between the important and unimportant things in life in order not to waste time on the latter. The important aspects concern people and relationships – and not material things. I also believe that you should 'never let the sun go down on your anger' because the person concerned may not be there tomorrow to be reconciled with. We were so lucky to have no regrets because they must add greatly to the heavy and tiring burden of sorrow when they are present.

I do not believe you can run away from, or permanently circumvent, grief. You may make a temporary detour which can be helpful, but eventually you have to find your way through the dark and painful tunnel to reach the light which really does shine at the far end.

It seems curious to me that people should be frightened of death since it is the only certainty in life and very much part of it. But now I do find comfort in the thought that when I die Nicky will be waiting for me if I ever reach heaven!

Countess Mountbatten of Burma

STEPHEN JOHN

I met Robert, my husband, when I was fifteen years old and we got married just before my twenty-first birthday in 1965. In 1967 we were blessed with a lovely daughter, Susan Jane, and, four years later, in 1971, our perfect family was complete – Stephen John was born.

We are a very close family with grandparents, aunts, uncles, cousins, all living close by. Family holidays and Sunday outings to places of interest were our life until the children came of age, when they preferred to do their own thing. Christmas and birthdays were always special in our family.

We encouraged both our children in everything they did and they did extremely well at school with all their exams. Stephen's greatest love was sport.

On Thursday, 8 June 1989, this perfect family was shattered. Stephen lost his life instantly in a car accident. He was a trainee baker in his brother-in-law's shop: his ambition had been to one day own his own shop and drive a Porsche!

Stephen had just 'fallen in love' with his girlfriend, Lisa. On this tragic evening he had decided to pop over to Lisa's house with two loaves of bread from the bakery for her mother. They didn't ask him to go; it was an excuse to see Lisa for a few precious moments. Thursday was his regular day for playing snooker with his father so this was his only chance to see her that evening. He was at Lisa's house for just a matter of minutes, saying, 'Can't stop; playing snooker with Dad tonight.'

The journey home took approximately ten minutes. It had rained all day after weeks of long, hot, sunny days. Stephen was halfway home when he had his accident, colliding with another vehicle.

As Stephen had not returned home from work, something told me to get in my car and go and look for him. A puncture, I thought, although all the way along the road I kept saying to myself, 'Please God, don't let me find anything nasty.' I knew he would be coming from his girlfriend's house because I had phoned to ask her if he had been there. She said that he had, but had left twenty minutes ago – this was what made me think he had broken down.

On approaching the scene of the accident I could see all the emergency service vehicles with their blue lights flashing. I jumped out of the car, ran across to a policeman I knew, and said, 'PC Mayes, it could be my son.' He held me back and tried to comfort me, still not knowing if it was Stephen who was involved. A doctor was driving away from the scene. I stopped him and said, 'Doctor, I am Sandra Rudd. It could be my son.' He said, 'Yes, Mrs Rudd.' I said, 'Please tell me he is not badly hurt.' He replied, 'I'm sorry, Mrs Rudd. It was instant; he knew nothing.' The doctor did not get out of his car, just wound the window down. He looked at the policeman and said, 'Can you take her home?' The policeman was kind, compassionate and sympathetic. In fact, I wrote to the Chief Constable later and told him how thoughtful this PC had been.

'If only.' 'Why?' 'How?' – words that will haunt me for ever. The 'if only' is very apparent because Stephen and his father always played snooker at 7 p.m., but on this particular day his father had changed the time to 8 p.m. because he couldn't get home in time. When my husband rang me to tell me about the change in time I had picked up the phone to let Stephen know, but then changed my mind because I thought it would mean he would just have an extra hour to wait when he got home. I felt very guilty. I now say to myself, If only I had let him know he might not have been rushing home to get here by 7 p.m. He would have had a bit longer with Lisa and allowed himself plenty of time to get home. I had even picked up the phone and started to dial his work number – why oh why did I change my mind?

Robert told me not to torture myself about it. He said, 'What if you had told him and the accident happened an hour later? You would have said, "If only I hadn't phoned him."' I thought about his remarks and they seemed to make sense. That night the whole family congregated at our home together with the vicar. Had this really happened to us? Yes, it had!

We have lived in our own bungalow since we married and I have been involved in the community for nearly as many years. Our house was an open home to many over the next few weeks, family and friends coming to offer their support.

One of Stephen's teachers phoned to say the whole town was in mourning. A lady phoned – she gave her name as Peggy – and said that we wouldn't know her, but the accident had happened outside her gate. She had been at the scene immediately and Stephen was asleep then and there was nothing she could do. I will be for ever grateful for Peggy's courageous phone call to me.

Over two hundred people attended Stephen's funeral. Our service was not morbid; we played two of Stephen's favourite records, Elvis Presley's 'American Trilogy' and one by Bruce Springsteen. We permitted flowers, but requested that donations be sent to our local children's hospital. We handed over £1,282 7p; a vital piece of equipment was purchased. I chose the children's hospital because I felt that Stephen had had eighteen healthy years and some of those children wouldn't make eighteen years. We also gave his weightlifting equipment to a local club. With the £100 he had in his bank we bought a trophy in his memory to be presented each year to his college to a worthy bakery student. The main trophy stays at the college and we buy a replica for the student to keep. This has now been done three times.

Robert took no medication and returned to work after four days. I was prescribed mild sleeping tablets, which I have now weaned myself off. I left my job, started another, left that, and am now in another.

I grieved very loudly indeed. There wasn't a person in Norfolk who had not heard of my Stephen. I sometimes wonder now if I was a bit selfish inflicting my story on complete strangers. My husband was just the opposite. It is only now, five years on, that he can talk openly as I do.

At first, the only people who could help me were those who had experienced the same tragedy, whichever way they had lost their child. Friends and family were superb and I don't know what I would have done without them, but I needed to relate to people who had experienced the same feelings. I knew of several parents in my town who had lost children, so I got in touch with them. They were all very kind and came to see me and vice versa.

Later on, turning my tragedy into something positive, assisting other bereaved families as I do now, helped enormously, although it doesn't dominate my life. I would never advise a bereaved parent about anything because we are all very different in how we handle our loss. All I can do is tell them what I did. I left all existing photos on display, but could not bring into the lounge one I had developed after losing Stephen. Even when I did, it took me months to look at it straight on. Once it was in the lounge I would obstruct my vision so that I could not see it. For example, sitting on the settee, watching television, a cushion would be very near my face, obscuring the photo. Stephen's sister, Susan, had some of his clothes to wear, as did his dad. Each grandparent and an aunt had a keepsake – one had his camera, one his purse and a pen, and his little cousin had a fluffy toy.

Christmas to me was the most painful time, probably because it goes on for so long. It was always my favourite time of year, so decided to do something entirely different to what we had done for the past eighteen years. We went to our daughter's for Christmas lunch. This was helpful, although it was a painful day and I was glad when it was over. The first anniversary, and his birthday, were the worst. It was then I realised that he would not grow old. I still can't really use the word 'anniversary' because I have always associated it with something nice. I just say we are four and five years on.

The strains of losing Stephen were mainly borne by the extended family – grandparents, aunt, cousin and sister. They were worried that we would not be able to cope. We gradually proved to them that we would pick up our lives, although it would take time, and some things would take longer than others. Routine things, like taking my mother to the supermarket every Friday morning, ceased. I do still take her occasionally, but there is no routine.

I felt quite angry, asking, 'Why Stephen? He was such a lovely boy.' I said this to my rector, but he replied, 'Why anybody?' That made me think I was being selfish. I'm not sure that anger does subside. There are occasions when I'm lying in bed and the reality suddenly hits me. I thump the headboard, still asking 'Why?'

I no longer feel guilty, although as well as the guilt I felt in not telling Stephen about his father's change of plan, only a few days before the accident I had said to him that he should be home promptly if he was supposed to be at the snooker club at a certain time, and I tortured myself thinking, 'Was he trying to get home too quickly?' But then we go through life always saying things to our children, advising and encouraging them. Never do we question it – not until something happens.

By accident I found out about The Compassionate Friends and went along to our Norwich branch. There I met the most wonderful person who became my saviour – Pauline Rackham, the Norfolk County Contact. We are now best friends. Sadly, she gave up the group, and I no longer attend.

Stephen is buried in our local cemetery and Robert and I go there most weeks to attend the grave. One particular Sunday when we went to cut the grass, place new flowers and wash the headstone, as I usually do when it gets dirty, our married daughter arrived at the same time, so we were all busy tending the grave together. At one point I accidentally threw water all over my husband and we all ended up laughing our heads off. What would Stephen think!

Our policy is to remember the eighteen years of very happy memories and not that one bad day.

Since our loss life has taken on a new meaning. If I see something I like, and can afford it, then I have it. We have also taken ourselves off on several weekend breaks, something we otherwise probably would not have done so frequently.

After the first three months of tense grieving I said to Robert, 'Well, what are we going to do? Are we going to go around feeling sad for the rest of our lives or should we try and do the best we can?' We decided on the latter. Everything we did for the first time was painful, but then the more times we attempted these hurdles, the easier it got. Robert has not been back to the snooker hall, but he has gone back to playing badminton and watching Norwich City Football Club. I do not think the wound will ever heal, but we are coming to terms with our loss.

I don't think I could personally convince another bereaved parent that things will get better because I have met some who say it never will. All I would tell them is that for me it has not got worse. I would tell them to remember all the good times that no one can take away. Every situation is different.

I always say time does not heal, but it does help you to cope. That wound, in my opinion, will never completely heal. You may go on for weeks feeling fairly confident then, suddenly, you will be vulnerable and collapse in a heap of grief.

I have been very positive over the last two years. For the previous twenty years I had done 'voluntary' social work, always helping others with a crisis, never ever thinking I would have one of my own. I have now managed to turn my experience of loss to good use. I write to every family I see in our local press who have lost a son or daughter in similar circumstances just to say, 'I know what you're going through'. Also, I did some research on how police officers could benefit from my experience, as I had heard from other parents that their experience with the police had not been as pleasant as it might. I drew up some recommendations on how the police might deliver bad news, a little more softly than it is sometimes done. I went on to make a police training video to teach officers how to deal with delivering bad news, and to cooperate with Norfolk Constabulary on road safety.

Robert and I have only one other child, one lovely daughter Susan. Susan was four years older than Stephen, and I do hope I did not overlook her, although I probably did. Of course, she had a husband and her own home to go to, but being so close to her brother she grieved as much as we did. I would probably say to bereaved parents regarding their other children, 'How are your children coping?', just to bring to their attention the fact that they are also grieving. I would never say anything outright because, as I mentioned, we all cope differently, but this question would be enough to make them think about this aspect.

My daughter wrote a lovely letter to Robert and myself several months after we lost Stephen, saying she had come through by seeing her mother and father being brave and not cracking up. My sister, who is a single parent with a ten-year-old daughter, suffered dreadfully. Stephen was her nephew, godson and best friend. They worked in the same bakery and shared the same sense of humour. She is much younger than I am, so was more on Stephen's wavelength.

A little girl who had looked upon Stephen as the male in her life, not having had contact with her father since she was three years old, was also dreadfully affected. Stephen used to play games with her. The first time she came to our house after Stephen's accident she asked if she could go to his room, where they used to play. Painful as it was, I decided to let her, and hearing her playing his mouth organ brought a lump to my throat, but I decided to let her carry on as she had when Stephen was here.

I do not go to church, or haven't done so for a long time, but I went the Sunday after Stephen's funeral and found it very, very painful, with so many people coming up to me expressing their sorrow. I believe, as my vicar once told me that my strength will come from Stephen and above, and it has.

Robert and I have nothing to reproach ourselves about.

Stephen had eighteen wonderful years and, to us, they were not a waste. If anybody had told me, six months prior to his accident, that I was going to lose him I would have said, 'Point me in the direction of the nearest mental hospital, because I won't cope.' However, so far, so good. No breakdown, although I have been lucky in having the support of so many people. Perhaps other families are not as fortunate as us to have this back-up, and they may suffer much more.

My life has changed greatly. I feel I live for today; tomorrow never comes. I have changed my job three times. I do not look too far into the future. If I take a new job I don't say to myself, 'Does this job have prospects? Is it secure?' I just think if it falls through in six months, so what?

Talking to other bereaved parents was my lifeline. I knew they would always have time to listen. I find writing beneficial; it has helped me. After three months I decided to write to any newly bereaved parents I either heard of or saw reports of in the local press, because I know that all I wanted was another mother or father to write or talk to me when I lost Stephen, so I thought others would think likewise. This proved to be good therapy for me and was 99 per cent well received by others.

The best way to remember happier times is to include Stephen in our recollections of the past and also the future. Robert and I now have a lovely two-and-a-half-year-old grandson named Daniel Stephen. It has given me a real lift to see Susan happy, and Daniel is very special to us. We do not look for similarities, but they are there. Daniel will grow up knowing about his Uncle Stephen. There is no doubt about that, although he is not a replacement for our son.

As for keeping Stephen's memory alive, it will never die. He was born to me and for eighteen years we were bonded, as was, and still is, my daughter Susan. I lived for my children. Some people have said, 'What a waste of a young man's life.' I tell them it wasn't. His eighteen years were in no way a waste.

We were privileged, as were others, to have known and loved him.

Since losing Stephen there have been numerous hurdles to overcome and, with hand on heart, and with determination, I believe we are well on our way to doing so. For instance, going on our first holiday. Quite soon after losing Stephen, only a matter of weeks in fact, we went on holiday to Dorset. It was a disaster – too far, too soon (for us). We spent most of our time sitting in the car sobbing, so we returned after four days.

Similarly difficult was cooking Stephen's favourite roast chicken dinner. I didn't do it for probably more than a year afterwards.

All these hurdles were things we had taken for granted. Well, you do. You don't expect to lose your children. Each one was extremely hard, that first time, but after the second and third time it does become easier.

There are still some hurdles we have *not* overcome. Robert has still not ventured into that snooker hall. We still avoid eighteenth and twenty-first birthdays, engagements and weddings, as these would always be attended by Stephen's colleagues and friends. One day, maybe, these will also be overcome, but if they are not, so what? I believe that in the last five years we have climbed Everest over and over again.

Everything we have done has been right for *us*, but we are all different and must follow our own instincts.

Sandra Rudd

DOMINIC

Dominic had been a beautiful child, with large brown eyes and a big grin. It was hard not to love him and, during his teenage years at school, he got away with murder, twisting the teachers around his little finger and doing very little work. At the age of twenty-one, away at college, he took his own life.

This child had been my special one, a boy after two girls in my first marriage. He was followed five years later by another son by my second husband. Although every child has a special place in its mother's heart, Dominic and I shared so much during his childhood. We both had a love of the natural world and would spend hours roaming the countryside, identifying plants and insects, turning over stones and logs and finding snakes and wood lice. He developed a love of photography and one of his precious legacies is his collection of albums containing wonderful jewel-like reproductions of the beauty he saw around him. The only time our love of wildlife diverged somewhat was when he bought a ferret, which I never could learn to love!

After this idyllic childhood, being generally indulged by everyone he met, I think Dominic found the real world a very hard place. He became aware of the cruelty of man to man, the injustices of the world and the alien sets of values many people live by, including sometimes his friends, who were often more interested in sport and beer than discussing apartheid in South Africa! Dominic also wore his heart on his sleeve. Full of love, he wanted someone to care for – and the girls he fell passionately in love with could not cope and repeatedly broke his heart.

Every parent who loses a child by suicide must wonder how they could have prevented this. It seems such a rejection of all the love and support over the years, such a degradation of all the effort put in to try to help him or her into adult life. But when I look back I remember how Dominic, so ill equipped to cope with a cruel world in his late teens, and determined to be independent of his parents, made his life miserable by setting goals he could not fulfil and churlishly rejecting any offers of help or advice. All his life I was aware of his vulnerability, regularly dreaming of his death and waking distraught. Perhaps I was arming myself for the inevitable.

When we were told of his death I wanted to die as well. Life without him was unthinkable – and yet looking round at the stricken faces of the rest of my family I knew I could not leave them. My husband was amazing. We would sit for hours talking and talking, letting it all pour out without thought, crying and holding each other. I think we have never been so close. I marvelled that I could still move about normally with such a huge pain inside. I knew that I would never be able to be happy again, never be able to laugh or enjoy anything. I felt that life was now just a road grinding along to the end, which I hoped would be sooner rather than later.

Two years later I find I have laughed, I have enjoyed this spring and summer, and I find the best way to describe the last year or so is to say that it was like a kaleidoscope. My life fell into tiny pieces and then reformed into a different pattern, perhaps not quite as beautiful as the one before, but certainly containing areas of beauty. I visualise myself walking along a causeway with a big ditch either side. The road is stony and occasionally I fall off into the ditch, but when I crawl back up I find I am still where I was and I can continue the pilgrimage. I give myself occasional pats on the back, reminding myself how well I'm doing with this enormous task, one I would have said I could never have coped with.

Undoubtedly, during the first weeks of agony the only thing that kept the family from collapsing completely was the brave, continual and sympathetic support of our friends. Never a day passed without a telephone call or a visit, some people calling almost every day to hug and weep and listen, others calling less frequently, but still willing to listen, while I, in particular, thought again and again about this unbelievable event, trying to find some explanation. They came bearing flowers, cakes, cards and even, in the case of one particularly perceptive friend, refreshing lotion for my puffy eyes. They talked freely about Dominic, letting me weep and weeping with me. They shared memories and brought photos. Dominic's friends came, usually in groups for support, were not embarrassed when I cried, and gave me precious bits of information about him to treasure. I will never forget these people. How very patient they all were, and not once did anyone suggest that I might pull myself together, dry my eyes and talk of something else. Only one or two friends could not stand the anguish, and for them I have great sympathy. Not everyone is able to cope with such anguish, and these people were right to withdraw to protect themselves. One friend in particular, very close to the family, arrived for the thanksgiving service and did not mention Dominic or what had happened. He behaved as though nothing unusual had happened. However, when I wept and talked about Dominic he was calm and unemotional and comforting in his way. I found that when people were unable to refer to Dominic's death it was painful, but normally once the ice had been broken by me they were only too pleased to join in with their own memories and feelings. It is difficult for people to know whether you want to speak of your loss, but from my own experience I feel sure that in very few cases is the opportunity to do so not welcomed with open arms – and fresh tears. The tears flowed freely and I would remember a friend who had always told me that a certain number of tears need to be shed and it is best to shed them sooner rather than later.

My closest friends grieved beside me, having known Dominic all his life, but one friend in particular, until then not one of my closest, became one of my greatest supports and confidantes. She would send pretty cards at regular intervals, just to say she was remembering us in her prayers. One other friend wrote that she was 'holding us in her heart' – a phrase I will never forget as it made me feel so cherished. One of the most wonderful things to discover, admittedly in a very painful way, was that so many people really cared for me and my family.

At Dominic's thanksgiving service his friends stood up and talked about him with great courage. Dominic was a committed atheist and we sang Beatles songs, which he loved, and had a jazz band. He would have approved. A collection provided money to plant a small wood in his memory on a piece of land in front of our house, and his ashes are buried beneath a rhododendron bush on a sunny slope. Already butterflies and blue tits are taking over and wild flowers are blooming in profusion. We are so fortunate to be able to watch new life grow in his memory and to be able to wander in this little area with friends who come to see how it is progressing. It has been a source of great healing.

In addition I had the support of a member of a wonderful organisation, The Compassionate Friends. The relief of being able to speak to another mother who had experienced a similar devastating loss was indescribable. The isolation felt initially, especially in the case of suicide, is total, and it is comforting to speak to another, apparently rational, sensible and normal human being to whom the same appalling catastrophe has happened. They are proof that there is life after death, that although life will never be totally the same it will one day be worth living again, unbelievable as it may seem at the time. I had a few comforting conversations with my befriender and some time later joined the organisation. I now receive a regular newsletter and it is still good to know that I am not on my own in my grief. Two years later I have found the strength to try to put back a little of what I have taken by contacting a couple of other mothers whose sons have taken their own lives, just to say, 'Hi, you're not on your own – I'm here if you need to talk.'

We speak freely of Dominic at home, often laughing about what his reaction to something would have been, and there are photographs of him here and there around the house. I have tried very hard not to display more of him than of the other children, but have taken pleasure in creating a collage of photographs in one frame. One photograph stands on a cabinet by the sitting-room door where it can be seen as people go in and out, but I have to admit that there are still times when I am feeling fragile and have to angle it away slightly.

A nightmare hanging over me when Dominic first died was the thought of having to dispose of his clothes and belongings. I foolishly spent a wet Saturday afternoon in the house alone sorting out his bedroom and ended up quite distraught. It needs to be done with a friend or relative, in small bursts and only when the time feels right. The amazing thing is that a day dawns when something impossible suddenly seems possible, without any apparent effort. It is important to listen to your instincts and respond accordingly. I found Dominic's clothes and belongings slowly filtered away – some given away, some thrown away, some kept to be treasured. Eventually the day came when my husband, my other son and I had a blitz on the last oddments and, rather dramatically, a wall was demolished to enlarge my younger son's bedroom by incorporating Dominic's. I found this traumatic at the time, but am now glad that I do not have a room to brood in. After all, Dominic's spirit must be out in the woods and fields he loved so much.

During the first year there are anniversaries to be struggled through, Christmas being the one most dreaded. None was so bad as the anticipation of them, although some tears were shed (and welcome letters and cards received). Dominic did not like Christmas, finding all the commercialism and general hype too much to cope with, and tended to come in on Christmas morning saying, 'Bah, humbug, Mother' rather than 'Happy Christmas', so this helped a little. The end of the first Christmas Day was welcome, however, and we were relieved to find we had some-how survived. On the two anniversaries of his death a group of his friends, about twelve in all, organised a dinner party where they drank more than they should have, regularly toasting Dominic and making speeches that became more and more incoherent, generally having a good time and remembering their friend in a way he would have enjoyed himself. Dominic's younger brother, Alex, was invited, and it was very healing for him and for Dominic's friends.

The emotions following the death of a child are complex. At first I felt no anger. I had rarely been angry with Dominic when he was alive, although sometimes exasperated, and experienced exasperation rather than anger when he took his life. I felt like saying, 'Oh Dominic, for goodness' sake ...', but also experienced great sorrow that he did not consider the effect on the rest of his family. The most overwhelming emotion was guilt. I disappeared under a slag-heap of guilt. Did I love him enough? Did he know I loved him? Why didn't I see he was distressed? How could I have missed the signs? Was I a *good enough* mother? Did the break-up of my marriage, when he was three (instigated by me), affect him more than I thought? – and on and on. Eventually, after two years, it was necessary for me to receive professional advice to help me cope with the guilt, and I now feel more confident about my mothering and feel that Dominic did take *his own* life, which it was his right to do, however painful for the rest of us.

It is easy to neglect siblings when a child dies. I was aware of the needs of his other brother and his two sisters, but had little extra strength to give support. I was moved and grateful when my younger son told me how, on his appearance in the pub the night after his brother's death, his friends risked their 'street cred' to stand and hug him. He went out every night to be with his friends where he could keep a hold on his life outside his grief-filled home. We missed him, but we understood. My elder daughter, who had a baby son, found great consolation in caring for him – grief caught her unexpectedly many months later. My younger daughter experienced the trauma of a divorce soon after her brother's death and had a very difficult time. She can still be a bit 'wobbly' sometimes, and we all shed tears together on occasions. I do not feel we supported our other children as we should have done, but honestly feel it is very difficult to do so when feeling so fragile and weak. Trite as the saying may be, time does inevitably heal, even when you thought it never would, and I have found it comforting to move into the situation of having happy memories to treasure, but without the sharpness of pain that accompanies very recent recollections. I was fearful of forgetting. Now I know that one does not forget, but the pain of memories subsides and happiness replaces it.

We who are put in this situation find it hard not to see it as totally negative, and it is very difficult to find any good in such circumstances. I find it comforting to know that Dominic was spared what could have been a difficult and painful life, that he died when he was young and beautiful, leaving me memories I can keep in my heart for ever, untouched by anything that happens to me, and that, ultimately, I have to admit that it was his life and he chose not to continue it.

A German friend of his wrote a wonderful letter, telling me that he felt that Dominic's view of life and death was different from anyone else's and that to him it was a small matter to open the door and walk through. Certainly death was very real to Dominic all his life, something he talked about without fear. I feel I have to respect his decision, but if there is an afterlife he will certainly have some explaining to do!

Val Golden

LIZ

Liz was lovely; she had red hair and hazel eyes; she was solemn, shy and bright. We had our son, Nick, when Liz was two years old. She loved him passionately until he started to crawl and blundered into her doll's tea party; then she wanted to send him back.

Two years ahead of Nick Liz marched off to primary school, and we can see her now, standing still and straight, playing the recorder at school concerts. We were so proud of our little girl with her two red pigtails and our fair-haired boy.

Nick and Liz grew up happily together, childish interests soon diverging, with Liz following fashion, experimenting with very mini mini-skirts, youth groups and 'best friends' and Nick seriously into fishing and ham radio. At the age of ten a friend introduced Liz to a local chapel, and at that early age she enthusiastically embraced the faith that was never to leave her, nor even to falter, for the rest of her life.

There were simple family holidays, mostly caravans and cottages in the West Country – no money then for fancy foreign flings. Later we discovered the Lake District, bought heavy boots and cagoules and tramped the fells. By now the pigtails had gone, and a curtain of shining red hair hung over the physics homework. Some time between 'O' and 'A' Levels, the red curtain succumbed to an expensive snip and blow-dry at a local hairdresser. A schoolgirl went in, and a young woman came out.

Her chapel played a big part in Liz's life but, to her regret, not in ours. At seventeen she was baptised there. Perhaps our children were too busy for teenage rebellion, because it never spoiled our family life. University studies beckoned, and there was the pleasure of seeing both our children set off in turn with a trunk in the boot of the car, complete with transistor radio and, of course, the obligatory guitar. Incredible to think that we were almost glad to be on our own again!

So much happened so fast – Liz's honours degree in physics, her twenty-first birthday and engagement in the final year to a fellow student from the North of England. Then came the postgrad year, the job search and the decision to settle in the Midlands, halfway between both families, so as to be quite fair ... and the magic and the hard work of the wedding and our son Nick's graduation the same year.

So there we were, such a lucky family, not financially well-off, but both children had good futures in prospect and there was the happy addition of Liz's husband to our family circle. Jobs and marriage meant that we were all living hundreds of miles apart, but frequent visits, letters and phone calls kept us close, with Liz planning that we should move to her village on our not-too-distant retirement.

Then, for Liz, suddenly, without warning, without symptoms, there was cancer. Not just cancer, though, but savage, all-invasive, terrible, diagnosed-as-inoperable cancer. It was a week before we knew – imagine that young couple together with their terrible secret, trying to protect us, the family. Words cannot describe the bombshell effects upon us all, Liz's brother by now one hundred miles north of her in Yorkshire, we, her parents, two hundred miles south in London. Friends must have tried to sympathise, but my abiding memory, after the dash to her bedside, is of desperate isolation in that bomb crater, not knowing the best way to climb out to help and protect Liz and her husband. I was filled with anger. I remember banging my fists on walls when alone, attempting to assuage the pain.

Ever since Liz's death I have been meaning to write 'Liz's Story'. I had been told that it was therapeutic, and had been given books written by parents like myself, charting in detail the last weeks or months of their child's life, with blow-by-blow accounts of the many and varied treatments, all trying to write away the pain.

All were moving and poignant to read. However, as I tried to tell the story of my brave daughter, from the first terrible diagnosis, through the chemotherapy and the many eventual operations, I knew that it would be too harrowing both to read and to write, and would have ended up the size of an encyclopaedia. There were so many emergencies, so many incredible recoveries and so many unbelievable indignities heaped upon this young, clever, hopeful girl who was my daughter. No. I couldn't write it then, and I can't write it now . . .

Liz died a very distressing death six days after her thirtieth birthday, and nine days before Christmas, in 1985. Although desperately ill, she had planned to spend Christmas with us, had even made puddings, and had wrapped presents for each of the family. After the funeral and burial in the village where she had lived, we travelled two hundred miles back to London with her husband and Nick. In shock, we acted out Christmas together, eating the puddings, and opening the presents. How did we do that? Now we cannot imagine it. We were robots then.

For all newly bereaved parents, Christmas, birthdays and the anniversary of the death are the most dreaded periods. For us, these were all hideously crowded together in those few cold December days. Because that first Christmas was so traumatic, the following year our son Nick pressed for a different venue, and we spent it in a friend's country cottage where we had enjoyed many holidays in happier times. It was right for us then, especially for Nick, but if we had had younger children still at home, with different expectations, I suppose that I would have had to try to be more traditional. Even our very grown-up son wanted to retain the special Christmas dinner, the wine and the familiar unwrapping of presents together. The desire to cancel Christmas was strong, but I found that it was not an option. Since then we have spent almost every Christmas together as a family, recognising the comfort that it brings, but always remembering . . .

For several years following Liz's death I know that I lived almost entirely with the memory of that cruel illness. Grieving, angry, seemingly inconsolable – gathering no comfort then from the memories of happier times – I sometimes felt at odds with my husband, who was coping quietly and more successfully than I was able to do. After nearly forty years of happy marriage, this was incredibly frightening. Sometimes so desperate was my sorrow, I wished that my life would end. I know that this thought comes at times into the minds of other bereaved parents, however fleetingly. Much later another parent said to me, 'I didn't want to die, but I didn't want to live either.' This neatly summed up how I had felt. It seemed so beautifully simple then – the only balm available when despair was at its greatest, and there seemed nowhere else to run to. However, I am sure my confused brain was telling me that, having solved the problem, I would soon be my old self again, and would then be able to get on with my life . . .

Those dark thoughts and the angry grieving produced great guilt, because it seemed that I valued neither my husband, nor our son. I knew that it would be difficult for Nick, as in addition to his own grief he had suddenly become an only child and thereby the sole recipient of all our love, hopes, fears and expectations. This is a fearsome burden for any surviving child and, even when there is more than one, I am sure that in such sorrow it is possible for us to give the impression that our lost child was somehow extra-special, perhaps even perfect – the golden one.

I was lucky in that Nick was always ready to talk to me about Liz, even though the distance between us meant long, tense phone calls. He encouraged me to telephone him at any time, even if I wanted only to cry, sensing perhaps that his father and I were grieving in very different ways. He was strong enough to admit that in those early days he too sometimes broke down in front of friends or colleagues, and was not ashamed of it.

A caring social worker at one of the hospitals where Liz had been a patient did her very best to help me. I did not recognise it at the time, but she was offering me just what I needed, which was to allow me to talk on a regular basis about all that was troubling me. I supposed at first that she was suggesting an occasional chat. Counselling was a word I had never heard. By the time I realised what was on offer I was finding it too traumatic to travel to the hospital in London where Liz had suffered so much, and I went so irregularly that I was not taking full advantage of this help. I regret that I did not see earlier that this was the first step on the path away from despair.

Was I doing nothing to help myself at this stage? During Liz's long illness I had seen a television programme about The Compassionate Friends, a self-help group for bereaved parents, and had hidden the address away, like a squirrel hiding a nut, knowing sadly that the day would come when I would need it. I wrote at once and within three weeks attended a very small group, but transport difficulties made it a problem to continue. It seems that for the second time I gave up too easily, failing to see the potential help available. Perhaps early shock and depression made merely venturing out too enormous an effort. However, I met a terrific County Secretary from the organisation who went on to write me long, tender letters, telling me from her own experience that things would improve. Of course I did not believe her, did I? After all, I had lost a very special, a very loving daughter. How could things improve? I had no religious beliefs to sustain me, and the lives of friends and relatives appeared to make things harder; their day-to-day comings and goings seemed unreal, trivial even, cocooned as they were from sorrow. I was probably not helping them to help me; I thought it would be obvious that I wanted to talk about Liz, and to hear them speak her name. Perhaps I closed up inside when they did not, imagining that they were embarrassed or even fed up with my troubles. How could I have thought that? Maybe it was unfair. Now I am more open and positive about my needs, and make it clear that I never want Liz to be regarded as part of history.

In what I now see to have been too great an isolation, I was finding consolation in letters sent in answer to one of mine printed in the The Compassionate Friends newsletter. The very first response was from a mother with whom I at once felt such rapport that, even after eight years, we still write regularly and warmly, although we have never met. At first our letters were full of anger at our daughters' suffering, but eventually we wrote of other things – of our families, our hopes and fears. Our letters now are a mixture of the serious and the humorous, but we always find that we touch on the bond that links us. My heart lifts whenever I see her familiar writing. There were also other poignant letters, and all were of help to me. We wrote frequently at first, and even now most of us keep in touch, especially at Christmas. It is revealing to see how we have all progressed and have each dealt with our loss in our different ways.

There were other moments of comfort, too. During her last months, Liz had started to sew an elaborate sampler. She died before it was finished, and at first I could not even bring myself to remove the needle from where she last left it. But eventually I gained much satisfaction in completing it for her. Although no needle-woman, I was encouraged by the result and, with the help of books and graph paper (and a big magnifying glass!), I designed and worked on another in her memory. It is, I hope, a permanent record of what Liz meant to us, and although a challenge, I feel it was well worth such effort.

The number of photographs and sketches of Liz that we displayed in our living room may have given the impression to some that we were reinforcing the pain of our loss. However, I have always been quite sure that, together with those of Nick, they are for us an important reminder of our once-happy family life. A long time ago I worked as a freelance artist, but after Liz's death failed miserably even over a period of five years ever to paint a single likeness of Liz from just one of those many photographs. Later, when I was coping more effectively in other ways, I succeeded in just a few days. This was immensely satisfying for me.

There were two important events that stand out in my memory of those early years. The first stemmed from the desire, common to us all, to have something special in memory of our child. I badly wanted to see Liz's name somewhere other than on a headstone – and on something less sad. Had I been allowed, I think I would have written Liz's name in large letters almost anywhere!

After donating a book with a special nameplate and photograph to The Compassionate Friends' library, I looked for something more permanent. To our delight, at the chapel that had meant so much to Liz, we were allowed to plant a shrub and raise a plaque in her memory. At a moving ceremony, at which an elder of the chapel paid tribute to her life and faith, we planted a philadelphus bush, the flowers of which had a special meaning for us all, as they had filled our house on her wedding day. Tending this plot, and planting flowers there, helps us cope with the fact that we cannot visit Liz's grave more than once or twice a year.

The second event happened almost by chance. Learning that the mother of a young girl buried next to Liz also lived at a distance, I eventually tried to contact her through The Compassionate Friends' newsletter. I was not successful, but heard instead from a young mother in my daughter's village who had just lost her baby son. She had not written as one might have expected to seek comfort from me, but to give it by offering to tend Liz's grave.

At first I was afraid to accept her offer in case it had been made impulsively under stress. When we met I found a young woman, close to my daughter's age and with the same Christian commitments, who, though new in her grief, and with her own baby's memorial a few miles away, was willing to reach out and help someone in need like me. The friendship that followed was like a bright star for me in those dark years, and continues to be so now in happier times. I cannot express how important this has been.

However, after five years, and despite these special experiences, I did not seem to be making much progress. Liz herself had been able to cope with her suffering more readily because of her faith; sadly, I still could not share it. Looking back, I feel that I was not making enough effort to help myself by taking some positive steps. Because we were past retirement age, I suppose I felt that we did not have much life to rebuild and, without realising it, I was still looking back at closed doors, instead of trying to find new ones that would open.

A chance questionnaire sent back to a research group trying to find the cause of ovarian cancer led to a young researcher recognising my despair. She telephoned, urging me to seek help from my GP, but I resisted, not wishing to admit to him what I saw as weakness. Dogged in her determination, this young researcher, who did not know me, telephoned again and again, eventually pressing me to take some positive action.

She gave me details on Cruse, the well-known bereavement counselling organisation, and the name of someone running a Compassionate Friends group a few miles away. Embarrassment engulfed me! How could I approach someone in TCF, an organisation to which I had belonged for so long? Guilt and pride would not let me; what would she think of someone in my state of hopelessness after five years? So her address stayed in my diary for another year.

I did, however, contact Cruse, feeling somewhat diffident, but anonymous. Cruse sent me Carol. Thank goodness for Carol. She encouraged me to talk of the terrible things that were haunting me about Liz's illness, insisting that she was willing to listen over and over again. It was such a relief to be encouraged to do what had hitherto seemed a self-indulgence.

Carol also recognised that the main thing that was holding me back was guilt. In addition to the fear that I may have been responsible in some way for Liz's death (a feeling that I believe is shared by many mothers in relation to their child's death, whatever the cause, and however illogical), she saw that for me the largest part of my guilt was caused by my feeling so devastated for so long, thus adding to my husband's burden. She put my own and his differing reactions to grief into perspective, and although I was finding it difficult to believe, insisted that I still had something to offer in life. Confidence began to return a little – I was not beyond redemption after all! It was clear that my husband and son were relieved at this small improvement in my mental state, and I then took what turned out to be a very important step.

Nick had long looked forward to spending a few days alone with his father, so when I saw that in 1991 The Compassionate Friends Conference was being held close to where Nick now lives in Derbyshire, I saw it as an opportunity for them to be together without having to worry about me. Apprehensively, even reluctantly, I made a reservation for the residential weekend, and approached it on the day in somewhat the same state of mind, almost regretting my decision. It seemed likely that it would be rather a morbid affair, with perhaps an excess of sadness and tears. Would I leave feeling more wretched than when I arrived?

On the contrary, I found comfort, understanding . . . and hope. Apart from the general social gatherings and meals together, there were many small discussion groups as well as poetry meetings, entertainments and countless other activities. I felt a little like someone who had been offered a huge box of sweets, and did not know what to choose!

I looked around and saw more than two hundred parents who had all suffered the same terrible tragedy as myself, and who were able to meet, talk . . . and laugh together.

The time passed so quickly, and I felt incredibly uplifted. I could not wait to relate it to Nick and his father when they came to take me home. The words of the TCF creed had come to life, and were more than words. As I write this, I am thinking, Oh dear, this sounds just like a PR job for The Compassionate Friends; but that is exactly as it was for me.

On my return from the conference, I followed the advice given to me by the young researcher more than a year earlier, and con-

tacted my local group. I joined at once, and found there friendships which helped me more than I could have believed possible.
I wish that I had not waited so long.

My husband decided to join us when we attended the 1992
TCF conference in Durham, and has come to nearly all our meetings since. I am sure that I can hear our son Nick cheering from
the sidelines at this!

At the Durham conference I was able to see in one particular
way how I had changed in the intervening year. At the first conference I had not known how to choose between the various discussion groups, so desperate had I been then to talk about every
aspect of my grief. A year later, my need for that particularly
valuable form of therapy was so much less that I was happy just
to accompany a newly bereaved and special friend to her choice
of discussion. Of course, not everyone can attend a conference,
and I mention it because for me it led to those important local
contacts that have made such a difference.

All of us who meet agree on the poignancy of dealing with the
possessions left by our child. Those parents who have lost a
young child, or an older child who was still living at home, will
probably be faced with the agony of a bedroom crammed with all
the latest toys or records, and cupboards full of clothes. For us it
was different, and was a process that stretched over a period of
years. When Liz left home she took with her many of her childhood treasures and other possessions, and naturally collected
many more during the following years. They were returned to us
at various times, and because I had so little control over the tim-
ing, receiving them often brought a mixture of both pain and
pleasure.

Our ties with Liz's husband, which had been very close during
the first year after her death, naturally enough began to weaken
as he tried to rebuild his own life. This was a difficult and painful
time – an added stress that all bereaved parents of married children must face. People deal with death in many different ways,
and there is bound to be pain if you feel that the memory of the

child you are missing so desperately is being handled with anything less than the greatest of care. It may seem like rejection;
you know that your child's partner must move on, and you want
him or her to be happy, but you are always longing for things to
be as they once were.

I will admit, but with no regrets, that I have kept almost everything that was returned. I wear Liz's gold cross every day, and
delight whenever possible in wearing the many clothes she made
or chose. The souvenirs from her childhood have memories for
her brother too, and we feel that if Liz kept them with her all
those years, then they deserve to be treasured by us now.

The exception will have to be the enormous quantity of university notes and books which came back fairly recently, prior to
her husband remarrying, representing so much hard work and
which we cannot bring ourselves to throw away. Nick has
decided that his sister would thoroughly approve if they became
part of his garden by being incorporated with his compost, thence
into the soil and thus not to be entirely wasted. It is an eminently
sensible solution, but I will allow my heart to grieve just a little
at the thought of that beloved red head bent so industriously over
them. Bundles of my own letters to Liz from the time she went to
university, together with very detailed diaries of our early holidays, came back from her husband at the same time as her university papers. Reading them fearfully at first, prepared for
renewed anguish, we realised with relief how lucky we were to
have so many lovely memories of our family. It is these memories, rather than those of the four tragic years of illness, which are
now uppermost in my thoughts, and which sustain me.

It will be clear that I took a very long time to reach a stage
when I had any positive thoughts at all, and could wake each
morning without a black cloud hanging over me. I have tried to
identify what I did that was helpful, and what were my mistakes.
I obviously missed some early help, and think now that I would
have benefited if it had been closer at hand. I now feel that I was
too hard on myself, blaming myself too readily for feeling the

devastation that was only natural, and which added to my feelings of guilt. Instead of feeling ashamed of banging my fists on the wall, I should have bashed a helpless pillow instead, and no doubt would have felt better for it! I was right in my instincts not to want to forget Liz by appearing to be 'getting over it', and it helped me to see her remembered on a plaque or in a book, and to feel that she is still an important part of our family.

During the first years, Liz's birthday and the anniversary of her death were so cruelly close to Christmas that they hardly seemed worse than any other days; they were all so black. Nowadays, knowing that there are very special flowers and messages on her grave on those anniversaries brings me a measure of peace and comfort. When we cannot travel there ourselves at that time of year we know that they will have been placed there with love by Nick and by our good friend in the village. On Liz's wedding anniversary in the summer we get great comfort and pleasure from going to the grave ourselves with flowers as similar as possible to those used in her wedding bouquet, and spending some time in that quiet village where she once lived.

Meeting other parents at TCF gatherings has been immensely important to me. I have found among them friendships that I would have valued at any time, even if we had not been linked by such tragic circumstances. I cannot pretend that there is no longer any pain, or that there are never tears and never anger, but it is easier now to move into calmer waters. For both my husband and myself, our grief has somehow become interwoven with the memories of all the joy that Liz brought us, and together with the love of our son Nick, it has become part of the very fabric of our lives.

Barbara J. Moyes

BRAD

It began in 1988. I had three children already, aged ten, eight and four; two boys, Greg and Bret, and Adele, our bonus little girl.

The realisation that I was expecting again was a total shock. I was on the Pill and we had no intention of having another baby. I knew I was pregnant for a while before I even let my husband, John, know. By this time I had been to see the doctor and had had it confirmed and the wheels were set in motion for the future birth.

To say we toyed with the idea of a termination would not be true. I don't think either of us could have gone through with it. It was a difficult start to even more difficult times. Telling the family was, I felt, an awkward occasion. Mum and Dad were not too thrilled, as they thought I had enough on my hands, but John's mother and sister were pleased. Things soon settled down, and it didn't take me long to begin to look forward to my new baby as much as I had the previous three. It meant buying new things as all Adele's had gone, except the cot. Strangely enough, I didn't buy a lot and only ever got to order the pram.

The scan at sixteen or seventeen weeks went OK – 'nothing abnormal detected', I think was the term used. It was shortly afterwards that I did not feel well; I was tired and felt very bloated and big. At each clinic visit I was told I was bigger than I should be for my dates, although this was not unusual for me – my second baby had weighed ten pounds.

We went on holiday in May, to Tenerife. I found the flight rather uncomfortable. When we arrived I kept out of the sun as much as possible. I was extremely tired and developed an awful, dark, itchy rash on the inside of my legs. I now wonder if it was significant in Brad's demise.

At the clinic I showed them my rash, but was admitted for bed rest anyway as I had become very anaemic, out of breath, and had swollen feet. This had never happened before. There were lots of other mothers in for rest, and this just seemed like a small hiccup in the scheme of things. I was monitored at regular intervals, but never offered another scan, which I think would have revealed Brad's condition, although I realised now nothing could have saved him. A kick-chart was mentioned to monitor the baby's movements, and I think I realised then he had not been moving much. I remember coming downstairs in the early hours and holding my stomach, willing the baby to give me the slightest kick.

On 11 July it was my eldest son's eleventh birthday and I struggled to keep it happy. He wanted to stay up until 11 p.m. as that was his time of birth. He would be eleven at 11 p.m. on the 11th. It was then my waters broke. I was only seven months pregnant. As soon as I was admitted they knew the baby was in distress as the waters were meconium-stained. I was on the labour ward all night and given oxygen. Things took a much speedier turn in the morning. I think I saw all the doctors going, with the notable exception of my consultant. The last thing they tried was to attach a monitor to Brad's head, but with no success and, as my labour had not been progressing, it was all stations go for an emergency Caesarian section.

I remember crying as I signed the consent form and wishing John was there. I noticed the theatre clock said 1 p.m., so I estimated Brad's arrival at about 1.30 p.m. I was told later they had to fight to resuscitate him and a nurse had to hand-ventilate him until they were able to transfer him to Newcastle as Darlington could not cope with his numerous problems. They knew he had hydrops (a condition that affects some premature babies, but which little is known about) as well as, other complications and that, short of a miracle, there was no hope.

He was christened with John present. I bitterly resented the fact he was so ill. They brought him, in a portable incubator to see me, but he was hardly visible. They took a photo of him holding John's hand. Owing to his condition he was very bloated and bruised. They had struggled to get him out.

I was receiving visitors, but received few cards as people seemed to think they should wait. My children made me some, which I treasure, along with anything I have to remind me of Brad, including a scribbled account of the daily treatments and agonies we went through in the Special Care Unit. They come out every now and again, still painful, but I need them.

Brad was born on a Wednesday. According to the saying, 'Wednesday's child is full of woe' – so appropriate in his case. John's cousin worked on the ward and must have known Brad's plight, but of course she kept quiet so that, when the urgent phone call came to say that Brad was failing fast, I was in a total panic. This was on the Saturday. John had been up to see him before this. I cried all the way in the ambulance, so sure was I that I would never see him alive. We rushed in and when I saw all the tubes, drips and monitors I knew things were very serious. They calmed me down and Brad rallied enough for some of the staff to return to other duties. Here at last was my son, looking bigger than he should be, owing to the excess fluid in his face, neck, tummy and even his 'privates'. He had thick dark, wavy hair and a dimple in his chin. He was mine, and I'd have laid down my life for him.

Here began a week I can only describe as 'hell on earth'. They tested both of us for all known causes of hydrops, but it is still an unknown quantity. He was on a ventilator all the time so I never heard him cry, but his little face would scrunch up in obvious pain at times.

I sat and told him of his family. He did get to meet his brothers and sister. It must have been a shock to them, but they seemed to accept it. My parents and John's family, for various reasons, never saw him, and we all find that sad. I phoned people, but there was never good news. Apart from John, I had no visitors, but the staff were good and I could visit the unit any time, although the short way was through the baby ward with all its joyful new mothers. I could wander outside, and I remember how hot and sunny that summer was.

I bought Brad a cheap yellow toy dog and that, with a blue hippo from a lady at John's work, were the only toys he had. They later went in his coffin along with our photos and a white dummy my mother bought (placed in his hand) and a small teddy from my brother who, with his wife, was the only one to see him in the chapel.

I went home on Friday as I knew my family needed me, especially my little girl. My friend took me up to see Brad on the Saturday and we went as a family on the Sunday, but I cried all the way home as when I looked at Brad I could see the light had gone from my darling little boy's eyes.

My mother and father had just arrived on the Monday when the last phone call came from the unit to say he was once more failing fast. I was frantic and we arrived just in time. He had always had one eye open, whether asleep or awake, and there it still was. I felt him going much colder and, by then, knew what the monitors were telling me. I told him it was time for things to be as he wanted, not for him to cling to life for our sakes, and his eye closed in a final goodbye.

They brought him to us in a private room. He was wrapped in a blue blanket and they had removed all the tubes and sticky tape. At last I could cuddle him properly, but never as I imagined. We have photos of this. It was so hard to part with him, but we had to, and I last saw him in a crib, being wheeled away. We never went back. We were given a booklet. I think it was called 'Saying Goodbye to Your Baby'. It gave a few guidelines for the funeral and contact names and addresses – later to come in useful.

Then followed a period of numbness. His funeral was on the 27th and my main memory is of the carpets of flowers that arrived and the huge yellow teddy bear, much bigger than the tiny coffin. I do remember the vicar coming to talk about the service and me asking if we could have the children's hymn

'Summer Suns Are Glowing', but he didn't know it.

I found it very hard to pick up the threads of normal life. I spent a lot of time in tears and found myself carrying one of Adele's dolls around as if to appease my empty arms. Somehow I was able to sleep, though not peacefully, and waking up with the realisation that I wasn't still pregnant and had no baby became a walking nightmare. I coped with the day-to-day housework and looking after the family, but they and I knew there was a large part of me missing.

I remember an incident about six weeks after our loss. We attended a wedding, probably my first venture back into social life. A friend's sister remarked on how well I was coping, saying she would have felt like going to pieces. If only she had known how I felt inside.

John was very good and patient with me, but for him it was all over and back to work. He came with me to the cemetery until the stone was laid and he felt that was enough. I did feel a bit bitter that he didn't miss Brad like I did. I was glad when Adele left playgroup as it held memories of being pregnant and people there didn't seem to be able to talk about Brad. Even I found it hard to speak about him; but I needed to do so. My mother was very good in this respect and we often had long telephone calls. I could talk to her like no one else. Meeting people who didn't know about our loss was very hard. I would start to tell them and then struggle to continue, but that was better than those people who chose to ignore Brad's existence. That hurt.

I went for a check-up at the hospital and burst into tears. It seemed unnecessary when I didn't have my baby. I ended up getting help from a very understanding lady doctor. She told me everything she knew about hydrops and got me a final discharge letter from Brad's unit. This came months later as it had been lost! I was able to see her as and when I needed to, and slowly I realised I was visiting less frequently and finally I stopped altogether. She eased my terrible feelings of guilt for ever having conceived Brad just for him to suffer so much.

I had joined SANDS (see pg 204) and The Compassionate Friends and wrote to lots of ladies in similar, and sometimes worse, situations. John had found me the information about SANDS, but there was no local contact or group. There is now, but I feel it is too late for me. I have worked through the painful early times with some good penfriends, all of us in similar situations. At one time I waited eagerly for the post and always replied straightaway. I have kept one or two contacts, but it is more social now. A lot of grief and pain went down on paper. I wrote to The Compassionate Friends newsletter and used their library to the full. John could not understand how I could read books in floods of tears, but I found it therapeutic. I took up learning to drive and passed my test first time. I wrote to myself about how I felt and composed a few poems, one of which was published in 'The Angels of the Heart' book.

I have a lovely sampler, made by a penfriend, which holds pride of place in my dining room. Photos of Brad are too private. He was bruised and covered in drips and wires. They are in a special Baby Blue album which Adele gave me, with a bluebird sticker on it. Adele was always so understanding. One photograph I carry in my passport so that he is always with me when I go on holidays. I wish I had had something which was his. Now hospitals offer a palm- or footprint, a lock of hair or cot-tags and wrist-bands. There will always be so many 'if onlys'.

So here we are, almost four years down the road of despair. It has become easier, but there are still dark times, thankfully much shorter. I call his grave his garden and don't go quite so often, but it is a focal point. I plant flowers in season and use silk ones in the vases – I don't like the fresh ones dying so quickly. He has his toys – tiny china ornaments and, at Christmas, a little tree. I had a dream a while after he'd gone. He was in the crib I had last seen him in and I was telling my mum to come and see him. I still knew he was dead, but he was moving and opening his eyes. There was someone telling me he was better now. In a more recent dream Brad was older and with my dad, who died last year. They were playing in Mum's front room and my dad was asking me if I knew who Brad was. Then I realised he was growing up.

In my mind I have him at two ages – as he might be now, and as he was. We have another little boy now, Luke, who was two in January. He was never a replacement, or even reminded me of Brad, but I often wonder why we had to have Brad only to lose him.

This is not the end of Brad's story. He will always be with me in spirit and, if only in my dreams, I can hold, love and cuddle him.

Goodnight; sleep tight.
God bless. Loved forever.

Anne Upex

KEITH

I had been married for thirteen years and had one son who was eleven when he died. My marriage was not especially happy and in September 1985 I decided to divorce my husband. I'd realised that I could cope and manage financially without him and that we – Keith and I – would be happier alone. I think it must have been the quickest divorce ever for, by December, I was clutching my decree absolute. Then, six days later, Keith was killed in a hit-and-run accident outside our house. He was my life and my world. I'd loved him so much (and still do) because we had been so close through many, many bad times. The upheaval of divorce was not so unbearable other than hurting my pride. Financially we were better off because I had full control of my monetary circumstances and knew exactly what was spent where and so on. I felt cheated of the good times we were just beginning to experience through my 'freedom' when Keith died.

I had learned to drive that year and bought a car once I had begun the divorce proceedings so that I could cope with daily life. As a child I had contracted polio which makes walking any distance a problem, especially if it is icy. It also became important that I could take Keith on treats. We went to local leisure centres and, if it was far enough from Peterlee, I would swim (I'm very self-conscious about how my leg looks) or I would watch him ice skate. We planned to go all over the area in the summer during the long six-week holiday.

We were just getting into a routine and we were happy. We felt relaxed and unstressed about where we were or how long we had been out. It was a relief to be free of his father's presence at home and yet there was a grief for the dead marriage. Most of my feelings were selfish and silly but I did feel lonely, or I thought I did. It was not until Keith died that I knew what loneliness was all about.

That particular Sunday was lovely. We were preparing for Christmas and had gone to town cleaning the house. Keith was an eager and efficient helper, almost as if he could speed the three remaining days away by his efforts that morning. We had lunch at Grandma's and then had a lazy afternoon. By teatime Keith had become bored with his own company and activities so he went to visit his friend across the field. He was killed returning home only ten minutes later.

I heard the collision but took no notice as I was busy finishing a piece of writing for Keith's godfather (also called Keith) in an Old English style. We were going to take it to Hesleden and spend a little time there with Keith C. and his wife. They were our favourite people and we have shared so many hilarious hours together.

There was much police activity on the hill so I could not get the car out to go to Hesleden and, besides, I still thought Keith was with his friend. I rang the other Keith to ask him to collect the work and by the time he came I was becoming agitated about my Keith's absence. I rang my parents to see if he was there and my father came down. I also rang my sister Kathleen asking her to keep me company, although at this time no one had confirmed what had happened. Finally, when my father told the police that my son was missing, he was taken to the local hospital. He identified Keith from his clothing and returned to tell me.

I could have told him that I had known from about 6.30. From that time I had had the most awful growing feelings of fear. When I voiced these to Kathleen she very sensibly said it was too early to tell; then, as time went on, she said, as I wept my fears, that it was looking more likely that Keith had been involved in the accident. Looking back, this was very brave and honest of her. If she had said that everything was going to be all right and that my fears were silly I might not have valued her as much as I do today.

When finally, at about 9.30, my father and Keith C. returned to break the news it was me who asked directly, 'It was Keith and he's dead isn't he?' It was the pain on his face when he came in which confirmed the feeling that had been growing.

Kathleen wept quietly; my father was ashen and Keith C. silent. I wanted to scream a denial of what I had heard. I also wanted to weep without stopping, but there were things to do. Keith's father and other close relatives had to be informed. I had to do something; I could not sit back and let others do it for me. This, I know with hindsight, was shock keeping me active. I rang my friend Pat with whom I taught and told her what had happened. I was very concerned that my friend Margaret, who was also a teacher at the same school, should not hear about it from the news broadcasts. Margaret was also Keith's registration tutor at school, as well as my closest friend.

My ex-husband was informed and travelled through the night to return to the area. He was very shocked and distressed, as much as I was. My family closed ranks and wanted to protect me, and cherish me all to themselves. They were kind and compassionate, yet guarded, even a little distant towards my ex-husband. My friends were wonderful to me and their attitude to David was similar to that of my family, so I was well supported whereas he was not so well 'cushioned'. At that moment in time we needed each other for no one else knew what we felt. As Keith's parents we each needed the support of the other.

The events so close to Keith's death are lost to me still. I cannot remember much after the phone calls I made. I can remember the duty doctor coming and being given a sedative once I had been put to bed in my mother's house. How I got there I do not know. I awoke to a low moaning sound, and tears were streaming down my face. The moaning was my own and the tears must have been flowing for a while as the pillow was quite wet. My sister had shared the bed with me and all night she had cuddled me. It was very early in the morning and we lay and wept together.

The next days were exhausting. The house was full of visitors and the phone never stopped ringing with calls from well-wishers. Who came I cannot recall, but I do remember feeling dreadfully tired and disorientated. Everything seemed remote and unreal. My body felt very heavy and moving seemed to take an effort. I could not think, let alone concentrate on anything; I just seemed to go through the motions of being awake or asleep. Certainly sleep did not refresh me nor make me relax. I had been prescribed sleeping pills which helped sleep come quickly, but they did not keep me asleep. I was restless and preoccupied with thoughts about Keith; the worst times were last thing at night and early the next morning.

I thought about Keith all the time and the tears would come and after the tears I always felt exhausted. I found that coping with the never-ending stream of visitors was difficult. I was so tired all the time, and the effort of hearing what they were saying was tremendous. My mind was not with them; all my thoughts centred on Keith and it was with a very conscious effort that I was able to participate in the conversation.

I could not eat and my weight shot down which, again with hindsight, helped cause the tiredness I experienced. I could not afford to lose weight at the rate I did as I had never been a well-fleshed person. I often felt dizzy in those early days of loss and tended to stumble. This was probably due to the fact that, initially, I was living on coffee and cigarettes.

My father and sister did all the running around that a death necessitates for I was in no state to do anything. There had to be an inquest later so there was no death certificate and Dad had to see the coroner to have the body released for burial. I think he found all this very difficult for he and Keith had enjoyed a very close relationship. My father had always wanted a son, instead of which he got two girls, so when Keith came along he was ecstatic. They went everywhere together, and if my childhood memories of a day out with my father are accurate then Keith's days would have been wonderful. I thank God that my father's hobby is photography because I have so many photographs of Keith. They are not posed ones; in each he is doing something and his attention is not on the camera.

At first I was distressed that I could not see Keith in my mind. I think I was trying too hard to see him and the photographs helped me visualise him. It did take a while before I could actually look at them without sobbing uncontrollably. Even now I sometimes cry when I see them, but at least I have been able to display some in the house.

Both my ex-husband and I were distraught on the day of the funeral. Much of the day is a blur except that both families supported us and the day went with no rancour or unpleasantness. Only the grief poured out and united us for the occasion. I needed David's presence and care – or I thought I did – in my hour of need. I needed one special person to understand my anguish and pain, and so did David, but his need of me as comforter seemed greater than my need of him.

I had stayed at my parents' home and found it difficult to return home to begin my life in new circumstances. I could not stay at my parents' for ever, and while I was there they would not grieve openly. They were trying to be strong for me and they were so concerned about me that I felt too protected. I stayed away from my home a while longer by going to stay with my sister, but as she had a young daughter of her own plus a demanding occupation it was a very temporary stay.

When I did come home I did not cope very well at all. The silence was unbearable and I was out as much as I could possibly manage. My friends were absolutely marvellous. I had been teaching at the same school for ten years and had made some really good friends. The school had a fairly low turnover of staff and most people had been there for lengthy periods of time. We used to socialise as a staff group and I have some good memories from my time there. It always seemed a happy school with caring members of staff.

Two in particular saw me through the worst of it. Margaret, a

spinster living alone who, although childless herself, certainly
knew about the loneliness angle, and Pat, my PE friend who pre-
tends that she is hard-hearted, gave me much support. Both gave
me love and time out of their busy lives. Without them and my
family I would not have made such a good recovery.

Pat called to see me more frequently than others and took back
progress reports while Margaret provided a retreat. We share
many similar interests and she had encouraged me to take a City
and Guilds course in Fashion and Design the year before. I
remember making a skirt at about that time, and of course it
would have remained unfinished if it had not been for Margaret's
help and advice. As I said, my concentration level was at zero, so
this skirt could have turned out to be unwearable, if not unfinished altogether.

I desensitised myself to being at home through this skirt. I
would go home to use my sewing machine and, because it was
something I enjoyed doing, I could manage short periods of time
alone. The silence did bother me, but I stuck at the task and it
helped to restore my ability to concentrate. I never stayed long
because I tired easily. I felt at that time that I could do nothing
successfully, so this skirt project boosted my self-confidence
when I needed that kind of reassurance. I felt that my life was a
failure. I had nothing to show for the last thirteen years. My marriage was over and I could not even lay claim to being a mother
any more. I wept for myself then.

I was full of misery and self-pity as the loss of my son also
meant that I would never be a grandmother. This thought gave
me a lot of pain and made me very aware of my own mortality;
when I died there would be nothing of me to carry into the future.

I went back to work far too soon and did not last a week. I
could not concentrate and I found I could not bear to see eleven-
year-old boys. It was to be some weeks yet before I could cope
with work and misery. I thought I was not coping because I was
so lonely at home. In desperation, I rang my ex-husband and
asked him to help me return to work and adjust to a childless

house. He came back for what became another difficult period. I needed someone at home while he needed the familiar and the comforting. He was out often, as had been my experience when we were married, and I felt used. He was in a no-win situation actually because I resented, really resented, his presence in the house. I did not want him near anything that belonged to Keith. I did not want him in my bed and I did not want him in Keith's bed. His presence in that room robbed it of its 'Keithness'. The smell of the room changed and yet, when he was at home, the unbearable silence and sense of waiting for someone to come home was eased. But this was not enough. It was not right and did not feel natural and, of course, David wanted my support in his grief, my help in getting through the first horror of it all until he could cope alone.

My deposits of strength were not vast on the emotional front and I needed them all for myself. We were not man and wife in the true sense; nothing sexual, for emotional and other reasons, could have taken place. We were two people locked in cells of misery and despair. My cell had the extra torture of wanting him to go away and feeling guilty for feeling that way and yet dreading being alone. I felt most strongly that he intruded on my own needs.

My family would not accept his presence now for they did not want him as a permanent feature in my life. I could not explain to them that I did not want a reconciliation. It seemed too hard to find the words to explain and to make them see that I was not too sure what I did want. I felt hurt by my mother's attitude because it was very much a case of choosing her support or David's and actually I needed both.

Once David had gone permanently I felt better. I could weep, scream or give vent to my feelings without having to consider his distress. At times when the distress became too much to cope with alone I used to bolt off to Pat's or Margaret's. Another reason for wanting David to be gone was that his attention was focused on the people who had killed Keith. They were unlicensed, uninsured and driving an unroadworthy vehicle which, rumour had it, was full of stolen window frames. He was outraged and angry at all of that, plus the running-away element. It is probably just as well that he lived away from the area because he could very well have done them some physical injury as his anger matured. I do not think that I could have coped with any trouble, especially of that sort at that time in my life.

The nights were still the worst time when thoughts of Keith would come drifting in unbidden to cause tears, and I felt very uneasy about being alone at night. Finally I committed a silly weakness. I allowed the dog to sleep on the bed. Her weight beside me was a great comfort but of course now the aged and spoilt animal is still sleeping in the bedroom because she has become used to it. She's cheeky too, and growls if disturbed! Actually, once I had let her sleep on the bed I felt a lot safer and do not really regret the decision. I am not sure what a miniature poodle could have done to an intruder, but her presence gave me peace of mind that I was not alone!

I had to go into the school several times because Keith attended the school where I taught. We had always travelled together and I cried and cried all the way down the drive the first time. This was another desensitising exercise suggested by my doctor. I feel that he was right, because there were some people who had not seen me since Keith's death and they took these opportunities to offer their condolences. I could not have accepted them and then gone about my teaching duties, for I was too emotionally upset. My absence also gave them the chance to express their shock to each other and to talk about the incident which they would have been unable to do had I been present.

I also visited my classes to thank them for their many cards and expressions of sympathy which they sent when they learned of the accident. It is worth mentioning that I received more cards from my less able children and those who came from the poorer areas of the town. A lot of the children at that school had problems at home and did very well despite them.

When I did return to work properly there were times when I felt heartily sorry for my colleagues. We bereft parents are keenly aware of how many innocent references there are to death in general conversation, and so too were these wonderful people. When someone made one of these remarks I could have wept afresh at their discomfiture. The number of bitten tongues and *non sequiturs* that occurred in the staff room that year was unbelievable.

Some friends avoided talking about Keith or even avoided me in the town centre. The latter did hurt but when I mentioned it to my doctor he gave me a positive way of looking at it. These people were afraid of offering their sympathy and thus causing me pain so they avoided me. This obviously was their way of coping with the situation in the most caring way they could. Then there were other people who on meeting me for the first time after the accident did offer their sympathies – these people were being very brave as well as caring. The only person I do not like to mention Keith to initially in a conversation is my father. I realise how much he still hurts when we talk of Keith and that hurts me too. I have learned that mentioning or not mentioning my son is all basically a matter of respect. Whichever course of action people take is motivated by respect, and I think they should be respected back for it.

As time goes by I have come to believe that time does heal. I will never forget my son, nor will I ever cease to mourn for him. At least now I am in charge of when I cry and have learned to control my feelings. At first it was totally the other way around, but I have come a long way since then. I think all people do heal but at a different level. Take a physical wound as an example: some wounds heal beautifully and eventually leave no scar; other wounds heal over but leave a festering mass underneath which may need specialist help to remove the infection, and this tissue will need longer to heal and may leave a permanent scar. Other wounds always result in scarring, but the point is that scar tissue is in fact healed tissue.

It helps to have good support, for no one would leave a wound unattended, and for bereft parents our support is like the dressing on a wound. My experience is that, like an old soldier's, my wound twinges now and again. It has to, otherwise it would mean that Keith did not mean much to me. I have to acknowledge that this wound has weakened me and I have learned not to become over-tired, for if I do I am likely to become distressed by bad memories.

I knew that within that first dreadful year any major decision I made could have been a disastrous mistake. In the March of the following year (1986) I met Richard. He was a bachelor, and again the support he gave me was tremendous, despite the fact that he had no experience of a child's death. He is, though, a rare and understanding person. He lived alone, and although he had done so for six years since his mother remarried he knew about loneliness which can be overwhelming. Earlier in the same year in which Keith's death occurred Richard's mother died. He was able to use this experience to empathise with what I was going through. It was so good and reassuring to be in his company. He coped with the tears and anger – the whole range of emotions that accompany grief – with such patience, strength and compassion. I felt such peace in his company.

I have been Richard's wife for five years now and we have a tiny daughter. This second marriage, for me, is better than the first because I feel valued and loved. My feelings for Richard are good, sound ones. They are not based on my need for comfort due to the bereavement. I think that if that had been so it would not have lasted this long. There is a good, mature feeling of love and concern for each other's well-being. Then there is Jenny, our much-loved daughter, who has done so much to help all the family recover. She cannot replace Keith, for no one can, but she does bring her own joy into our home.

I am writing this in the kind of quietness I once thought was lost to me for ever. Richard is working at his drawing board and I can hear the occasional swish of his marker on paper, and in the distance, from a neighbour's garden, I can hear my little one's voice as she and her friend hunt for worms! Life is good and I think I am very fortunate to have not only a second marriage but our small girl. Second chances in life like this are very precious. I can enjoy the comfortable quietness of this day and remember my son with no distress, whereas once the quietness was suffocating.

I do think that anyone marrying a bereft parent is taking on a lot, and there are many more things for them to cope with, so the commitment to that person has to be one hundred per cent certain. I also think that the bereft person, in their vulnerable state even two or three years on in grief, has to be very sure of their motives for remarrying. I honestly did not want a partner simply to father another child. She was conceived accidentally, but she has brought such joy with her. Richard dotes on her and she on him. I love seeing them together.

Yesterday I attended the funeral of one of Keith's friends, Philip, who was killed in a traffic accident last week. Anne, his mother, is in the same position that I was in six years ago, and I do feel for her. As yet she does not know how hard the road is but I shall be there whenever she needs me.

Carol Winn

STEPHEN

Compassion is one of the most precious faculties of the human heart. In taking pity on the sufferings of a living being, the person forgets himself and understands the situation of misfortune. By this sentiment, he withdraws from his own isolation and acquires the possibility of uniting his existence to that of other living beings.[3]

Leo Tolstoy

We were a close family unit, always caring about each other. Grandad lived with us and we all adored him. Sunday lunch was always special as it was the only time when we would all be together to talk. Both of the children were musical and also active in sport. Janine played netball for County and Cambridge and Stephen played hockey and cricket for the Old Williamsonian Club. Stephen also loved motor racing and would often take his camera to Brands Hatch to take photos of his favourite cars.

Thursday, 8 November 1990 was a normal, busy day. Janine was at university, Stephen was on day release at the local technical college. When we came home from work Stephen was there playing chess with one of his friends. We had tea and then Stephen said that he was going to the Bull Hotel as he had been asked to do bar duties that night. He enjoyed doing this work as he met a lot of people and it was sociable.

Just after midnight our doorbell rang. We had gone to bed quite late. We thought Stephen had forgotten his house key. When I opened the door there was a policewoman standing there. My first reaction was that something had happened to Janine, as she was away. When the policewoman shook her head I realised that something had happened to Stephen. 'An accident,' I thought. 'He's in hospital.' Never did I think for one moment that the worst that could happen had happened. All I can remember the policewoman saying was '. . . he was pronounced dead at . . .' My Stephen. Gentle, caring Stephen – dead. No! No!

I cried and cried. John went into Grandad to tell him. John cried and cried. Grandad was too shocked – never said anything. The policewoman cried. How was I going to tell Janine her brother was dead? I had to go to her. I telephoned my sister-in-law and stepbrother and asked them to come round – I didn't say why. They came immediately. The policewoman broke the news to them. By this time I was in overdrive. I became very organised and practical and was comforting John. My stepbrother drove us to Cambridge. We arrived at about 2 a.m. at Janine's flat, which she shared with two other girls. I ran up the iron staircase to the top flat and repeatedly rang the bell. A frightened voice asked who was at the door. I said, 'Janine's mum.' Immediately the door opened. I ran to Janine and hugged her and told her what had happened. She could not believe it. Not Stephen. We all cried together, arms wrapped around each other. Her friends made us a cup of tea and then packed some of Janine's things into a bag. They said that they would inform the college of what had happened and that we were not to worry about that side of things. We arrived home at about 5 a.m. Janine insisted on going to see Nik, Steve's friend, to tell her what had happened. Nik didn't know. She was devastated.

The police came and asked if two of us would go with them to identify Stephen. I couldn't face it. I was frightened of what I might see. John thought he should go, but really didn't want to. Eventually it was agreed that John's brother and my stepbrother would go. When they came back my stepbrother told me it was Stephen and that he looked peaceful. I began to telephone people and just hoped that the media would not report the name over the radio before I could contact immediate family, but that wasn't to be. My mother and stepfather heard it on the radio, as did my niece, who was on the coach travelling to London to work. Extended family saw it on television that evening.

People came and went. Some brought shopping. The police came again, this time to obtain statements from John, his brother and my stepbrother. The policeman was very kind and very sympathetic. John had become the strong one while I just kept crying. We now know that a fight had broken out in the hotel bar and that Stephen, along with others, had been trying to stop it. Stephen was fatally stabbed by one single knife blow. The knife went straight through his heart. He didn't know anything about it. His death occurred in less than a heartbeat. Three other men were stabbed and were treated in hospital. A girl was injured by the girlfriend of the man who killed Stephen. She had to have three stitches in her head.

Saturday morning, and masses of cards and letters had arrived. Each one of them made us cry. So many people were saying so many lovely things to us about Stephen. That day, family from far and near began to arrive to share their grief with us. The CID came too, as did David, our vicar, who arrived during a quiet interlude and seemed to offer a little bit of calm during a period of chaos. We asked David if we could sit in the church that night, just the three of us. We needed to be alone together, somewhere quiet. Somewhere the telephone would not keep ringing, where people would not keep knocking on the door. The doctor offered tranquillisers, but I didn't want anything. I preferred to go through this at my own pace. Somebody from Victim Support came, a very nice young woman who listened to us. A very difficult assignment for her, I think. Late on Sunday evening the police telephoned us to say that someone had been charged with Stephen's murder. The enormous sense of relief brought on by the fact that this person had been caught was quite overwhelming. I don't think I could ever have rested if the person was still out there, somewhere, possibly to kill again. During the rest of the week cards and letters came pouring in. The phone rang continuously. Flowers arrived almost every day.

Every minute of every day my consciousness was filled with Stephen. I had a physical pain in my chest. There was an empty void. I had lost part of me. The baby I had cared for and protected twenty years had been snatched away from me. I'd sit in his room, go through his books, tapes and photo albums, hug his clothes – I could smell him. I began to pick up his guitar and play a little. Tears would stream down my face. It was so painful to go shopping. I couldn't be in the shop too long – I wanted to go home as soon as I got there. I would see Stephen's favourite food and tears would well up – I had to get out.

I was very grateful to family and friends who offered us Sunday lunch for several weeks. Cooking was such an effort. I had no interest in it at all. Housework did not get done for weeks. The little bit that was done was done by a friend who came twice a week. I began to think life wasn't worth living. That John and Janine and Grandad would be quite all right without me. All I wanted was to be with Stephen, but there was a part of me that said I wasn't thinking straight and that my family needed me. They were all grieving; all of us here emotionally battered.

I began to gather together photographs of Steve and put them in an album. This album was special. It began with his birth certificate and the many cards of congratulations we had: Steve's christening with the names of his godparents; his first birthday cards; the first Mother's Day card he made at nursery school; all the class photographs up until he was sixteen years old; the many happy holiday snaps; his 'O' and 'A' Level certificates and many other things special to Steve. I also wrote several poems. I found it very therapeutic to write these verses. They just seemed to flow straight out of my head and I had to write them down quickly.

I went back to work two weeks after Stephen's murder. I needed some sort of structure to my day and my work gave me just that. I wasn't able to complete a full day for a long time as

my concentration span would not let me. Also, I was very forget-
ful and constantly tired. I was very apprehensive on the first day
back as I didn't know how people were going to react to me. I
arrived very early, before anyone else, as I didn't want to be con-
fronted by a sea of faces. As those who work closest to me began
to arrive I went up to them in a way that gave them permission to
say something to me or just give me a hug. One of the managers
gave me a bunch of freesias. There were others from different
departments who came to offer their support, offered to take me
out to lunch. All these wonderful people helped me get through
my first day. There were some who avoided me for many
months. Eventually they told me that they hadn't known what to
say to me.

The weeks went on. Christmas was the last thing I wanted.
The presents, decorations, office dinners, parties and cards. I was
just not interested, but I felt that presents and cards were
expected. I could not bear the thought of Christmas cards being
sent without Stephen's name on them. However, Stephen had
been developing into a wonderful photographer and had taken
photographs of snow scenes around Rochester. One of them was
of Rochester Castle. We decided to have two hundred prints of
the castle processed and then spent many evenings gluing them
on to card and inserting a flysheet with Steve's name, acknowl-
edging his work.

The mother of a very dear friend of mine suggested that we
spend Christmas with them. We did just that, but when it came to
giving out and opening presents I could not bear it. I went into
the kitchen and sobbed until it hurt.

Christmas came and went and Stephen was still in the mortuary. I telephoned the coroner's office many times to ask when
Stephen would be released, but they would never give me an
answer. January passed by, then February. One day, in March,
when we were sitting in the undertaker's office, chatting to the
sympathetic lady who ran it, the telephone rang. The voice at the
other end of the line said that Stephen had been released and he

could be collected. The utter relief we felt was quite overwhelming. We had got him 'back'. No one could mess about with him any more. At last we had control; he was ours again. After just over four months we could bury him. We had all that time to decide how we wanted Stephen's funeral to be organised. We spent a lot of time thinking about the music, the prayers, the readings, flowers and donations in Stephen's memory.

The choice of charity for donations to be sent to was very important as it had to embrace handicapped children and music. Stephen was always a willing volunteer, raising funds locally for children with disabilities. The charity we nominated was the Nordoff-Robbins Music Therapy Centre in London. The charity received so many donations that they set up a fund in his memory, and when they moved into their new premises in September 1991 a therapy room was fully equipped with musical instruments from this fund. The room is known as Stephen's Room. We were deeply touched by the kindness of the charity and the generosity of Stephen's friends and our family.

Stephen's funeral took place on 14 March 1991, a bright, warm, sunny spring day. All the hundreds of daffodils planted along the roadside were blooming. The crocuses covered the grassy paths like a carpet. It seemed as though all the Medway towns came to say goodbye to Steve. There were masses and masses of flowers. The centre of our town was brought to a standstill as the funeral cars made their way from St Nicholas Church to the cemetery. The love and support that came from so many people helped to get us through the day. Everyone hugged us and had something to say, including the big, dark, chunky bouncer from the Bull Hotel, who said 'Great bloke!' as a tear ran down his face. We still had many hurdles to get over. The court case was just one of many.

During the next few months we discovered The Compassionate Friends and the sub-group, Parents of Murdered Children. I sent for literature from them and read everything they sent. I searched bookshops for appropriate articles to do with murder, unexpected death and bereavement in general. We both became volunteers within Victim Support and began to talk to local groups about the practical and emotional effects of the aftermath of murder. Eventually we participated in the training of Victim Support volunteers who wanted to help families of murder victims.

Stephen's twenty-first birthday was on 12 October. It was a terribly sad and empty day. Nobody sent a card or letter. Just a 'Thinking of You' message would have meant so much. For someone to acknowledge that Stephen had existed was all that we wanted. Late that night my sister-in-law and stepbrother arrived with a bouquet of flowers. I just burst into tears. They said that they had felt such a terrible sadness and could not begin to imagine how we would be feeling.

The trial was approaching. Through Victim Support we heard about the Maidstone Crown Court Witness Service. I talked to the Coordinator who was very helpful and kind. She invited us to the Crown Court prior to the trial to see the layout – where people sat, what the procedures were – and explained how they could look after us and the witnesses. We both knew that we had to go to the trial. We had to be there for Steve, and in any event we wanted to know the truth about what had happened. I needed to know the injuries Steve had received. People do not understand this need, but it is very, very important to know what happened.

In November 1991 the trial for the murder of Stephen and the injuries caused to four other people took place at Maidstone Crown Court. It lasted three weeks. The girlfriend of the offender was given an eighteen-month custodial sentence, fifteen months of which were suspended. The offender was found guilty of injuring two people with a knife and given nine years for one offence, four years for the other. The third charge of wounding was dropped because of a technicality. The jury were unable to come to a majority decision for the main charge of murder. I knew something was wrong as the jury were out for about four hours.

The judge told the jury that they had given him no alternative but to dismiss them. I could not believe what I was hearing – what was to happen now? I put my hands over my face, began to cry, and then ran from the courtroom into another office and began to shout and hit the cupboards.

In January 1992 a retrial was held at the Old Bailey, in Court Number 1. We had to queue with the tourists to get into court. There were only thirty-two seats available in the public gallery. We managed to persuade the usher to reserve the front two rows on the right side for us.

Again, volunteers from the Maidstone Crown Court Witness Service supported us. I really do not know how we would have managed without them. I certainly was not strong enough to stand up for myself and ask for what I wanted. The retrial lasted six days. There was only one charge to be considered – murder.

The jury retired – one hour later they were back and ready to deliver their verdict. The foreman stood, looked directly up to the public gallery and, when asked to state the decision of the jury, said Guilty. The offender was sentenced to life imprisonment. No minimum recommendation was given. We had many friends and family supporting us and we all broke down and cried through utter relief – twelve other people who were complete strangers agreed with what we already knew, that he was guilty.

Almost immediately I went to pieces. I literally could not swallow. The doctor could not find anything wrong. He said that it was the effects of the trauma causing the symptoms and suggested counselling. I approached my vicar who immediately agreed to weekly sessions. I found them to be very beneficial and very gradually the 'swallow' became easier.

Soon John and I became very active within The Compassionate Friends. We became National Contacts for the Parents of Murdered Children and eventually I became Kent County Contact for The Compassionate Friends. This activity gave us a purpose. Befriending and helping others helped us too. I was working a full day by now and was able to cope with all the day-to-day problems associated with my job. My priorities have changed. Material things mean very little to me. Trivialities irritate me.

Three and a half years later I can say that I have done things I thought I would never do again. For example, I thought I could never laugh again, sing again, plan things again, but I have. I never thought that the physical pain in my heart would lessen, but it has. I still do have flashbacks and I still cry, but then I know I always will.

Irene Baldock

DANIEL

In April 1982 I was looking through the *Be My Parent* book (a book containing details of children needing adoptive parents) when my attention was caught by a lively looking Afro-Caribbean three-year-old called Daniel. The article described him as being bright and responsive, but severely disabled with cerebral palsy. It concluded, 'Daniel's new family must realise that no one knows how he will develop. What is certain is that this enchanting, sunny, lively child would have his best chance of all with a loving family's constant care, stimulation and encouragement.'

As a white, single woman with no previous parenting experience I was certainly not a social worker's ideal candidate, but I was the *only* candidate and I was persistent and so, in due course, I adopted Daniel.

We certainly had our share of difficulties as we adjusted to life as a family. I had given up my job, moved to a new town and into a tiny one-bedroom flat in order to take Daniel and, with hindsight, it was probably not a good idea for him to move in at the beginning of the six-week summer holiday! Daniel was immature, insecure, needed constant attention and, at four and a half, he slept very little at night. However, we overcame the early problems and, young as he was, he showed total commitment to his new family and he flourished. He still maintained contact with his maternal grandmother and aunts and uncles and saw them at least once a year.

He grew into a strong, healthy, sociable and articulate boy with a great sense of humour. He got on well with adults and children. Despite severe physical disabilities he became an enthusiastic member of beavers, cubs, scouts and the Red Cross. His great passion was football and he was a dedicated Watford supporter, attending all their home matches. Very slowly and painstakingly he learnt to sit unaided, feed himself, drive an electric wheelchair and use a special computer keyboard.

At eleven years of age he transferred to weekly boarding school as there was no suitable secondary school in our area. I was very distressed about this as I would never have considered boarding if there had been any other alternative, but Daniel rose to the challenge and loved it from the beginning, primarily because of the improved social life it gave him. During his first term he proudly announced his love for classmate Jane, but he coped bravely when Jane abandoned him in favour of Jason Donovan!

During his first year at secondary school I became concerned at the deterioration in Daniel's condition. He lost the ability to sit unaided, he became unable to feed himself or use the computer. He had very painful muscle spasms in his neck, arms and legs and couldn't sit for very long. He went into hospital for tests in October 1991 and was diagnosed as having dystonia secondary to the cerebral palsy.

Gradually over the next year Daniel's quality of life became more and more affected. He was in a great deal of pain and had to spend much of the time lying on a mattress on the floor both in class and at home. It became harder and harder to take him out because of the unpredictability of the spasms. We would still go to Watford, but sometimes he was unable to turn his head to watch the football.

In October 1992 Daniel was in terrible pain from spasms and his breathing was affected as his spasms were so intense they were cutting off his airway and he was unable to swallow. He was taken into the intensive care unit of a specialist hospital for neurology. He was ventilated and after two weeks had a tracheostomy. For three months he was kept paralysed and sedated and woken every third or fourth day to see if any of the drugs he was being given were having any effect. We must have gone through this process twenty-five to thirty times and each time, within a few hours, or sometimes it took the whole day, Daniel's body would be racked with such severe spasms that he would have to be resedated.

It was during this period that the doctors began to impress on me that Daniel's condition must now be considered life-threatening. On first hearing this I felt overwhelmed with panic. I knew nothing of death or dying, except to know that I couldn't possibly deal with it. I could not, would not, watch my child die. I could not believe it was happening. Daniel had always been so healthy and strong; perhaps the doctors were over-reacting, perhaps he should never have been brought to intensive care. As I tried to calm myself down I realised that there were two things worse than Daniel dying. The first was that he should have to die alone, without my support because I didn't have the courage to be with him, and the second was if he ever found out that he was dying. I remember telling myself over and over again that I had been involved in all the major events of his life since he was three. I'd helped him with any difficulties he'd had to face and now I must face *this* with him. I tried not to think too much about his chances of dying because if I had dwelt on that it would have incapacitated me, and I had to be with him at his bedside each day and be of some use to him.

After three months there seemed to have been a slight improvement and in January 1993 we were able to omit the paralysing drug so that Danny could be awake during the day, but he still needed huge amounts of sedation to keep him comfortable. The only remaining option was brain surgery. Daniel, who had always been terrified of operations, now had to face three brain operations and for the second part he had to remain awake. It was very hard to support him through this.

The operation had only a thirty to forty per cent chance of success, but at first things looked hopeful. We were able to take him off sedation; he came off the ventilator and started to sit in his wheelchair for short periods. Then we had further distressing news. It seemed that the operation had adversely affected his tongue movements and his swallowing mechanism. He might never be able to eat or speak again. This was a terrible blow, but at least his spasms were less severe and we began to plan our transfer back to the children's hospital and looked forward to this with eager anticipation.

We moved in early May and within a day or so the worst of the spasms returned. Daniel suffered terribly over the next couple of days as the nurses and I struggled to manage him on an ordinary ward without intravenous sedation. Daniel had a gastrostomy operation on the third day and on the fourth day was transferred back to intensive care at the neurology hospital.

During our short stay at the children's hospital Daniel also developed septicaemia. One of the consultants talked to me in the corridor outside the intensive care unit and asked me if I had talked to Daniel about dying. I reacted angrily to this. I said I had not and that I did not intend to. People do recover from septicaemia and I felt it was my task to keep alive in Daniel the hope that he would get well again. Despite my brave words I was deeply distressed by the implication that I should have been preparing Daniel for the fact that he might die. It upset me that I might be failing him in this because I wasn't strong enough to talk to him about it.

Daniel had always had a terror of death. I had always put this down to the many losses he had experienced as a young child. He was removed from his natural family at ten months. He had a foster placement which failed at two and a half years and he experienced a profound sense of loss when he left his children's home and moved in with me at four and a half. When he was five his social worker, who was his main carer in the children's home, was killed. Daniel would never go into a cemetery or graveyard and in his early years with me worried that I was going to die. I could not consider telling him he might die. It would only have added absolute terror to his already considerable mental and physical suffering. Daniel could not talk for the entire time he was in hospital because of the tracheostomy so there was no way that he could discuss his feelings, his fears or his worries. Books I have read suggest that children and young teenagers should be told that they may die. In Daniel's case I hope I was right in thinking that it would have been unbelievably cruel to have done so.

Returning to intensive care was a very traumatic time for both of us. Daniel was no further forward than he had been six months ago. I felt that the medical staff in this unit could not accept that Daniel had deteriorated. They had spent six months trying to get him well enough to leave and they could not believe it was necessary for him to return within four days. Without even bothering to ask what had happened, one of the consultants told me that they were expecting to transfer Daniel out again in a few days. The implication seemed to be that either I or the staff at the other hospital had panicked and engineered Daniel's return! Of course, Daniel never was transferred because they soon saw for themselves the full horror of the return of his spasms. For the rest of our stay we received a high level of support from the staff on the unit, and this is what makes it so painful to recall their attitude on that occasion. It really felt for a few days that they were writing Daniel off as a failure and wanted him moved out as quickly as possible so that they would not have to face the consequences – namely his eventual death.

There was only one remaining option and that was to perform the three-part surgery on the other side of the brain. The operations were postponed twice because on the eve of each operation Daniel was found to be septic again, but finally they were completed.

The second brain operation was not successful either and there was nothing further, medical or surgical, that could be done. There was a new problem as well; Daniel's veins had had so many lines inserted into them that they had become blocked and the doctors didn't know how much longer they would be able to find venous access for his drugs. Without the high levels of drugs he was on his situation would be unbearable; we would not be able to control his pain. The doctors felt that, in view of all these factors, it would be inappropriate to treat the next infection with antibiotics and they wanted my agreement.

I had been totally involved in every detail of Daniel's condition, every detail of his care. I often knew before the doctors told me what the next step would be, but I was totally unprepared for the shock that I might have to decide when he should die. I suppose I thought that we would go out fighting; that when he died it would be because the most aggressive medical treatment could not save him, not because we allowed him to die from infection by withholding antibiotics. I thought this only happened with elderly people, or people who were brain-dead, not mentally alert fourteen-year-olds. As I struggled to make this terrible decision I felt I was betraying Daniel. I would sit at his bedside talking and smiling normally, go out into another room and discuss how we were going to let him die, and then return to his bedside. I tortured myself with thoughts of what it would have done to him if he had known what we were doing.

I remember clearly the meeting on 2 August, my birthday, when I told the doctors I agreed that we should not treat the next infection. In my anguish I believed that Daniel would never forgive me if he had known what I had done. I was also terribly anxious that now that this specialist hospital had decided there was nothing further they could do for Daniel they would want him transferred somewhere else for terminal care. It was with the greatest relief that I heard the consultant's assurances that Daniel could stay on the unit until he died. It had become unthinkable that he should be looked after anywhere else.

The doctors and nurses were totally supportive of the idea that Daniel would never know that our goals had moved from cure to palliative care. From his viewpoint nothing changed from that day. I told him that all the operations were completed; there would be no more surgery. He was greatly relieved at this. I said that the next step was to adjust the drugs so that we could get him completely comfortable and that this might take some time. The nurses, my family and I then concentrated our efforts on salvaging what quality of life we could out of whatever time remained.

Despite being unable to talk because of the tracheostomy, Daniel formed the strongest of relationships with the nursing staff. They loved him for his courage, his wonderful smile, his great sense of humour and his love of hospital gossip! They tolerated his insatiable demand for football and wrestling videos and his commitment to Watford Football Club. They welcomed his family, his friends and even his dog! Nothing was too much trouble if it could contribute to Danny's physical or mental well-being.

During this time we were able to raise Daniel's drugs intake as high as we needed and a period of stability followed. He amazed us all. He came off the ventilator and started sitting up in his chair for several hours. We even managed to take him outside on short walks. On 18 August the nurses had arranged for the Watford goalkeeper to visit the unit. He brought with him many gifts, and when I came on the ward that morning Daniel was barely visible, grinning broadly under a mountain of Watford merchandise. Sadly this turned out to be Daniel's last 'good day' and as usual the crisis developed without warning.

On Friday, 20 August my sister went in to visit Daniel in the morning. He had been so stable for fourteen days that I had been planning to go away for the weekend for a badly needed break. At lunchtime on that Friday I received a phone call from the ward sister telling me that Daniel's temperature was very high and his spasms were worse. As I packed a bag and prepared to rush to the hospital I received a phone call from a friend telling me that she had arranged for Ian Wright, the Arsenal footballer, to visit Daniel on the Monday. When I got to the hospital Daniel was feeling very ill. He had a very high temperature and he was sweating profusely. I told him about Ian Wright's proposed visit and, as I watched his face light up, I knew he might not live to see it.

By the next morning Daniel's condition had deteriorated further and the registrar on duty that weekend, who I had not spoken to before, came to see me to tell me that he thought the time had come to start Daniel on diamorphine. If we did not take this opportunity to let him die of an infection we faced a nightmare scenario of not being able to get his drugs into him in the future. I shall always remember our conversation because what he said meant a great deal to me. He said how sorry he was and how he realised that what were just words to him were so much more to me. How grateful I was for this acknowledgment of the pain that all of us who loved and cared for Danny during those dark months felt, as we reached this point of no return.

The doctors expected that Daniel would die within twenty-four hours, but in fact it took a week. The nurses found me a bed in the hospital so that I could stay with him. On Tuesday evening he woke and I asked him if he would like me to read the sports pages to him and he indicated 'yes'. He listened for about half an hour and then fell asleep. It was the last communication I was to have with him. By Friday morning he was unconscious. During this last week, while logically I should have wanted the end to come as soon as possible, I never did. Mesmerised by the monitors at times, I felt only great relief whenever they started to pick up. Even at this late stage, when only one outcome was possible, I could not wish him dead. Given the choice I would be sitting there still.

On Friday evening, 27 August, Daniel died peacefully without recovering consciousness. I was sitting on the bed holding him; my mother and sister were holding him also. The four nurses on duty that night gathered behind us. The line on the heart monitor went flat and a few minutes later I asked the staff to turn off the ventilator. In its own way it was rather beautiful. I helped the nurses to wash Danny and we dressed him in a shroud. While we were doing this rigor mortis started. In a strange way this helped me in that I knew that Daniel's body was now an empty shell and he was no longer there, and when they came to collect him, to take his body to the mortuary, I was able to let him go without additional distress.

We had wonderful support from the nurses that night as we had had throughout our stay, but it was hurtful to me that the Senior House Officer on duty that night, who knew Daniel well, disappeared after writing the death certificate rather than speaking to me as requested. It is now four months since Daniel died. Although I find it upsetting to write about my feelings I can now do so whereas at first I would have found this impossible.

The most overwhelming aspect for me has been the guilt I feel. I know that much of this guilt is irrational, but that doesn't stop me feeling it. In the early weeks after Daniel's death all I could think of was that I had only one child to look after and that I couldn't get him past fourteen. I had to blame myself for that for who else was there to blame? I couldn't blame the hospital staff because I knew for sure that they had done everything in their power to help him. I felt a tremendous sense of personal failure and worried that I might fail in other areas of my life, such as work. I felt guilty because I had contributed to his death by withholding antibiotics. I felt I had killed him and so betrayed the trust he had in me. I tortured myself by thinking that he would never have understood what I had done and that he would never have forgiven me. I even told myself that I couldn't have loved him enough or I wouldn't have been able to do the things I did.

Worse was to come. A few weeks after Daniel had died I remembered that when I was told at the beginning of August that there were now concerns that we might not be able to get a line into him to give him drugs, I thought that I might actually have to kill him. If Daniel was to be in unbearable agony with no way of relieving his pain, I would have to do something. I had learnt a lot about the machines and monitors in intensive care and I remember thinking, if there is no other way, have I learnt enough to end his life without him knowing what I am doing and without increasing his suffering?

I have read many books and articles about bereaved parents and I have usually been comforted to find I am not alone in what I feel, but I have not read about anyone else who felt that they may have had to end their child's life themselves because they had reached a point where his suffering could not be relieved. This has been the hardest problem for me to deal with because it is not something you can talk to the doctors about. What I really need to know is whether in the event of Daniel's suffering becoming unbearable they would have ended his life or whether I would have had to. I can't expect any doctor to answer that.

Facing up to the physical and mental suffering that Daniel endured is also immensely painful. The cruelty of what happened to him, the unfairness of it all and our powerlessness to change any of it, are like physical pain. The misery of his last year seems to block out memories of happier times. It worries me sometimes that I won't be able to let go of all the pain and misery because they are all I have linking me with him.

In the time immediately after Daniel's death there were things that people said to me which did upset me. The happy release theory received pretty short shrift from me! Yes, it was true that Daniel's suffering was over, but there was a much better way – he could have got better! There certainly wasn't much happiness around as I watched him die. Secondly, I became terribly upset by those with strong religious beliefs who thought it would comfort me to be told that Daniel's death had been part of God's plan; that there was a reason why it happened which would become clear later. How could I accept that a loving God had deliberately planned Daniel's suffering and death and that by implication this was somehow OK because He had a reason for it! In the early weeks I felt compelled to question this reasoning and eventually achieved some peace of mind by reading a book from The Compassionate Friends' library entitled *When Bad Things Happen to Good People*, by Harold Kushner. This reassuring book reaffirmed what I was desperate to believe, namely that this tragedy was unplanned, undeserved, bad luck and the natural consequence of the complex brain damage Daniel received at birth. There was no reason why it happened and if some good can come out of it, which it surely will, then this will be a consequence, not a cause.

I knew nothing of dying or death, bereavement or grief before I lost my son. When I say how hurt I feel when some people avoid talking to me about Daniel I remind myself that before this happened to me I would not have known what to say either. I, too, would have worried that I would upset the bereaved person by talking about their loved one. I now know that the opposite seems to be true. Daniel is undoubtedly my favourite topic of conversation.

One unexpected aspect of my bereavement was the strength of the ties I had with the staff of the hospital. For ten months I saw more of the nurses than I did of my family or friends. We were united in doing the very best we could for Danny and when he died my contact stopped. I did go back a couple of times to visit, but something strange had happened. That group of people who had laughed, cried and suffered with us and had allowed themselves to show their love to this young boy, who had discussed with me the terrible decisions we had to make, supported me through the darkest of days, could not talk to me of those things after Daniel died. I was desperate to discuss my feelings with them, but the opportunity never arose. I do think it would have been helpful for the hospital to have provided some sort of follow-up service for me.

Daniel died at the end of August and, almost immediately, it caused me to worry about how I was ever going to get through Christmas week, which was also his birthday week. I told myself that it would be easier to bear if I could look back at previous years and think what a wonderful time he had. But the last two Christmases and birthdays had been spent in hospital with Daniel suffering terribly. My memory of Daniel's last Christmas Day is

the time it took to sedate him and put him out of pain as his
spasms became uncontrollable. I remember his birthday, when he
felt so low that he burst into tears when the nurses brought a cake
which he could not eat and which only reminded him that this
was supposed to be a happy day. The unfairness of it all was very
hard to bear. I knew that if the situation had been reversed I
would have wanted Daniel to have the best Christmas he could
manage. I did get a tree for myself and decorated a miniature
tree, instead of flowers, around the spot in the churchyard where
his ashes are buried. Worrying about Christmas and his birthday
was worse than the actual event. I knew it would be difficult, but
I got through it.

Unexpectedly, New Year was much worse. I could not bear the
thought of leaving 1993 behind because it was the last year in
which Daniel was alive. I suffered the first of recurrent periods of
depression which tended to last several weeks. During these
times it is as if I am reliving the horror and the pain of Danny's
suffering, but without the hope. There was always hope before.
At first, I hoped that he would recover, then I hoped that he
would live, and when I knew he would not I hoped that I would
get him home for a weekend, and finally, once he started on the
diamorphine and there were only days left, I hoped each morning
that he would not die that day.

I did see a counsellor from Cruse a few months after Daniel
died. She was very sympathetic and concerned, but I did not
really find the sessions very helpful. I think that the only support
I could accept at the time was encouragement to express my feelings and for these to be accepted and reassurance given that it
wasn't surprising that I was in such a state, considering what we
had been through. Instead, there was a tendency for the counsellor to try and make positive statements. Unfortunately, I found
this rather annoying and tended to argue against them. Some
examples of these positive statements are: 'It's quality of life that
counts, not quantity' – Daniel had neither for the last two years,
so this wasn't too helpful; 'His situation was so desperate it was

a good thing he died when he did'– if you are talking logically this may be true; when you're talking about feelings, it's not; 'You should look at it that you did well to get him to fourteen.' – I felt very indignant at this; I don't know any parents of healthy children (which Daniel was until the last two years) who feel a sense of achievement because their child hasn't died.

The counsellor felt that I should express all my feelings of guilt, betrayal and anger in a letter to Daniel. She had never counselled a bereaved parent before and she found it difficult to understand that I could not write to Daniel saying that I had considered I might have to kill him and that I had finally withdrawn antibiotics and allowed him to die. I would not have talked to him like that when he was alive and it would have seemed like a denial of our relationship to have done so now. I knew I had to express these negative feelings and was frequently doing so, but not in the form of a letter to Daniel. I did write a letter, as she suggested, but I did it in the way I would have communicated with him when he was alive, so I told him how much we all loved him, how much we missed him, how we admired his courage and his humour. I reassured him that none of what happened was his fault and that nobody could have fought harder, or more bravely, than he did and that many, many people would never forget him.

By the end of the sessions with the counsellor I was beginning to feel pressurised into seeming to feel better, otherwise it looked as if she hadn't done a good job. I have found it more helpful to talk things over with friends or other bereaved parents, because they don't feel under the obligation to make you feel better. There are things that have helped. I treasured the cards and letters that so many people sent to me. It became important that other people valued Daniel too, and I was grateful to the many people who overcame their worry about saying the wrong thing and showed their concern in this way.

Daniel and I were fortunate to be befriended by the former chaplain of his school. He became very close to Daniel during his time in hospital and he conducted Daniel's funeral service. Many people have said it was the best funeral they have ever been to. As the vicar said, 'Danny would have settled for nothing less!' I was so glad I taped the service. I have listened to it many times and found it very comforting. It was a real thanksgiving for his life and a really positive experience for me. Two further memorial services were held; one at the hospital and one at the school.

I was helped tremendously by The Compassionate Friends. I contacted them when I knew that Daniel was terminally ill and I found their publications very helpful. I have been slowly working my way through The Compassionate Friends' library and I've been reassured, if somewhat surprised, to find that so many other bereaved parents have had similar feelings to my own. I have been greatly comforted by going to group meetings and being able to express my feelings in a supportive environment. At these meetings we can talk freely about our children and our pain. It doesn't matter if we cry.

I was lucky to have four close friends with whom I could share my most painful thoughts. These friends did not feel that they had to come up with any answers to try to make me feel better, but they listened, accepting that they could not change the way I felt, but prepared to share some of the pain with me. My family, too, have offered unconditional support during Daniel's illness, death and the period afterwards.

I have found that writing about Daniel has helped. At first I could not write about my feelings so instead I wrote accounts of Daniel's illness and paid tribute to his courage. As the weeks went on it was helpful to express my own pain and fears and hope that, just as it helped me to read of other people's experiences, it may help some other person to read how I felt.

As well as writing, other creative projects help. I have designed and nearly completed a tapestry cushion cover which has nine small squares, each representing an interest or an important event in Daniel's life. It seems to be a way of thinking about him in a less painful way. I also found satisfaction in raising money for the Dystonia Society by selling Daniel's belongings or by other fund-raising activities. I also try to increase public awareness of dystonia as most people have not heard of it.

No one could have predicted that Daniel would develop a life-threatening disorder. In that I took my chances, like any natural parent, but how thankful I was, even through the darkest days at the hospital, that Danny had his own family to love him, support him, fight for him and finally, when he and I had to concede defeat, to hold him while he died.

I did not know that it was possible to live as I lived for ten months, beleaguered by suffering, pain, fear, panic, continual crisis and cruel disappointment and yet supported by the love and strength of others, finding strength in myself that I did not know existed. I know the painful feelings I now have must be faced and dealt with and that if I accept, as I surely do, that everyone else did the best they could, and all they could, for Danny, then I must find a way to believe that this applies to me too. I have to try to restructure my life without him. I must do this in memory of Dan who taught me so much. He never opted out of life because circumstances were not to his choosing and, in the most desperate situations, he showed an enthusiasm for life, a sense of humour and a love for people that are unequalled in my experience. I can only hope that he left a little of this behind as his legacy to me.

Jan Aldous

GARY

I lost my beloved son, Gary, in a car accident in Israel. We had only just returned to England after spending a holiday with Gary and his Swedish fiancée, Susan, who he had been with for two and a half years.

My eldest son, Stephen, broke the news to me and my husband, Roy, as Susan was the one to ring England with the news and, obviously, did not want to ring us direct. It was like a nightmare; it did not seem true. Later on we had a phone call from the British Consulate in Israel asking us if we wanted Gary buried in Israel or for his body to be flown home. We told them we wanted Gary's body brought home. Stephen flew to Israel with his friend to bring Gary's fiancée back to England and also to collect Gary's belongings and arrange for his body to be flown home.

Gary was our youngest son. He was twenty-six years of age. We were a close-knit family, full of loving and laughter, and Gary idolised my grandson, Daniel, his brother's child, always asking after him in his letters home. We learned that Gary had died instantly of a broken neck. There were five boys in a small car and Gary's American friend, Stuart, who was an only son, also died of the same injury. People, family and friends called at the house all day to offer their condolences and the phone was ringing constantly. One of the first feelings my husband and I experienced was 'denial' expecting somebody to ring and say somebody had stolen Gary's passport and that he had not died after all. We experienced so many emotions and such physical pain.

The funeral director visited us to sort out the arrangements. I

wanted the hymn 'Jerusalem' played at the service as Gary loved
Israel so much and this seemed appropriate.

Six days after Gary died his body arrived back in England. We
were not allowed to see him straightaway and his body was taken
to the funeral parlour. Gary's fiancée and my son arrived on an
earlier flight and they waited for the plane to land with Gary's
body as they felt it was something they wanted to do.

The next day we had to go to the funeral parlour as someone
had to formally identify Gary. I could not bring myself to go in so
my husband and Susan went. Even then I still felt it was not true,
but when my husband and Susan came out crying I knew it must
be. Eleven days after Gary died we had to go to an inquest which
was opened and adjourned for further reports from Israel, but
there is one thing that sticks in my mind and that is the really
kind words the coroner said to us: 'Mr and Mrs Wait, I want you
to know that Gary never suffered; his death was instant; he
would not have known anything about it.'

The next day, after the inquest, we went to see Gary at the
funeral parlour. I wanted to go with my husband and my sister-in-law. I think it is up to an individual to make up their
minds if they want to see their dead child and, for me, I was
not going to believe Gary's death unless I saw him. At the
same time I felt so nervous. I sent my sister-in-law and my
husband in first and I kept asking, 'What does Gary look like?'
They said, 'Peaceful; like he is asleep.' I was horrified and so
upset when I went over to the coffin where Gary lay. He was
dressed in a shroud and he had a veil over his face. He looked
like something out of a horror movie. Why could the funeral
directors not have liaised with us? Gary was a jeans and T-shirt
person and there was no need for a veil over his face. His
beautiful curly hair was all straight and had been slicked back
with grease. My husband kissed Gary and kept asking me to
kiss him, but this was something I could not bring myself to
do. I knew if I had done so and he felt cold I would have just
gone crazy. Even at this stage I was still in denial. Also, it was

twelve days after Gary had died, and even though he had been embalmed in Israel he did not look good. I try to describe this to myself and others as being like when you pick a flower from the garden – every day it dies a little bit more.

The next day, Gary's funeral, was just a blur. Stephen wanted us to wear bright colours as Gary would have liked this, but that was something I could not bring myself to do. So many people were there and all his friends walked behind the funeral car to the end of the road. It made me feel so proud; one of his friends' fathers said he had never seen so many young men cry at a funeral. On a card accompanying Susan's red roses she had written a verse that Gary liked to sing when he went out from Tel Aviv to the country. It was so beautiful:

> *I'm happy being happy*
> *I'm happy being free*
> *I'm happy being happy*
> *I'm happy being me.*

Gary's Italian friend flew over from Italy and stayed with us for a week. Everyone came back to the house after the funeral but I just wanted to be left alone so I could shut myself away. When Stephen brought Gary's belongings home from Israel his friends and his fiancée made up an album from the photographs they had and called it 'His Happy Album'. They said they did not want anything sad to be put into the album, such as obituaries. I can remember when we came home from the funeral Susan shut herself in the bedroom with this album.

The days after the funeral were just more of a blur. My strongest feelings were of hatred towards the driver of the car. When Stephen was in Israel he went to see the other two boys who were injured – friends of Gary. He also said he had to see the driver of the car, but he didn't know why. I asked him what he had said. Stephen replied that he had said Gary was a really quiet boy. I asked him if he had said he was sorry, but he had not. I

asked Stephen how he had felt and he said that when he looked at
the driver he hated him for the accident.

There were only fifteen months between Gary and Stephen
and they were not only brothers but friends. I could not understand why my husband did not feel this same hatred for the driver
and I began to resent him for this. I found that when Roy and I
were alone we would sit down together and talk about Gary from
when he was a baby to him being a man. I used to call this 'Our
Gary Time' and it helped us. One of the strongest feelings we
both experienced was that one of us would willingly have laid
down our lives if Gary could have been spared. In fact, we used
to say this to people. We have been married a long time and have
had a happy marriage, but, at the end of the day, a child is borne
out of the love of two people and is someone really special.
Children are your future; you expect them to go on and repro-
duce their own children. When you lose a parent, on the other
hand, it seems to follow the pattern of life, be more natural.

I rejected my other son, Stephen. I just kept on and on all the
time about Gary until, in the end, my daughter-in-law, Stephen's
wife, and my husband both made me see sense. My husband
asked me what I was trying to say. Was I wishing it was Stephen
and not Gary? I told him that was not what I wished, but he said
that was what it sounded like to them. Gary was gone and
Stephen was still with us. I should think about what I was doing
to him. Stephen's wife told me that when Stephen first heard that
Gary was dead he had been distraught and had asked why it had
been Gary and not him. Sometimes, when he is driving, he has to
stop and pull over as he cannot see for tears.

After six weeks Gary's fiancée returned to Israel, taking
Gary's ashes with her. It was her intention to scatter them there.
She kept looking at them and crying, 'My beautiful Gary in a
box.' Seeing her off at the airport was like saying goodbye to
another link in the chain.

The next week I went back to work, which was very hard.
It was most distressing when people just ignored my bereave-

ment, never mentioned it or just asked how I was and then stared at me. I found at first I could not cope and kept breaking down. Some days I did not want to get out of bed, but life goes on and I had to try to live a normal life for the sake of my family. Deep down I knew it was what Gary would have wanted. I always remember what somebody said to us – 'I know how you feel. I have just lost my father.' His father was ninety-three. Also, lots of people said I was lucky because I had another son. It would not matter how many children I had; it does not fill the void in my life.

Nine weeks after Gary died it was his birthday. That was so hard, sitting in the crematorium by the tree we had dedicated to him, crying, 'Gary, why did you leave me? If you could see the pain and heartache left behind.' You even blame the child you have lost for putting you through this grief. 'Why did you go to the kibbutz that day? You went to visit friends and you got into that car and now you have paid for it with your life. I just keep thinking you would have been twenty-seven today – so young to die. It was Susan's birthday five days ago and she rang me from Israel and said she felt devastated. Today she rang us and said she went out to scatter your ashes with friends, but she could not bring herself to do it. I told her we would do it together when we went back to Israel.'

My own and my husband's feelings towards each other changed. We were terrible, snapping and shouting at each other. We were grieving, but not together. I even went to the doctor to talk to him about it. He asked if we had a good marriage and he said some couples have been known to divorce over something like this. I really felt I needed to talk to someone outside the family and, in desperation, I rang the Samaritans. They gave me the number of The Compassionate Friends and, eleven weeks after losing Gary, I went along to one of their meetings. I wanted to be able to talk to other bereaved parents, to know I was not the only one to have lost a child. I also thought it would help to meet parents who had lost a child in the same circumstances. My husband would not go with me so I went with a friend, as I felt initially that I could not walk into the room alone.

To be able to talk about your child, to laugh, to cry, to vent your feelings even months or years on, is such a relief. I found that when I lost that feeling of hatred I was able to counsel other bereaved parents and I took on the job of fund-raiser for our group. As somebody said to me, 'Gary would have been proud of you trying to lead the quality and quantity of life he would have approved of.'

Gary did not have many possessions. Material things did not mean much to him, but I gave his snooker cue and other items to his friends as something to remember him by. I have all the letters I sent to Gary while he was abroad. He kept them all, which made me feel good. We have photographs of Gary on display; some we had in the home before he died and others we have added since. Also we had an oil painting of him and I often stand in front of it and talk to him. I always put flowers by it when I can; I would like to pass this down to future generations of the family as one of the strongest feelings I have is that I do not want Gary forgotten, even when I am gone.

Four months after Gary's death his friend, who had been sitting next to him in the car, came to visit and stayed with us. I went through a really bad time then and kept asking him over and over again what had happened. Why? I also felt a really strong resentment towards him because he was sitting next to my son in the car and yet he survived and Gary was gone. Other people I have spoken to about these terrible feelings say they are natural. Deep down we are looking for someone, anyone, to blame. My husband and I used to fantasise about things to do with the accident. I used to dream that Gary changed places in the car; that he had forgotten something and got out of the car then, when he got back in, he sat in a different seat. These are also common feelings.

Six months after Gary died it was Christmas, our first Christmas without him. I wished it would all go away. I knew I could not stand too much noise so I asked my son if he and his wife and my grandson could go and have Christmas dinner with her mother. I know he was hurt and puzzled, but they went. Susan and Tommy, another of Gary's friends from Italy, came and on Christmas Day we sat around Gary's tree and took him special flowers. This seemed to help. On the anniversary of his death, his birthday, Christmas, Mother's Day, Father's Day, I always take special flowers and sit by the tree with his father and my other son and his family. Father's Day will always have a special meaning for us as this was the day we learned of Gary's death. At Christmas, birthdays and the anniversary of his death I burn a special candle by his portrait. I would say to people, from experience, you should do whatever you want to do, whatever makes you feel right, even though you may get funny looks from friends and family. Some people keep their child's clothes for a while. I did, for a few years, then I gave some to charity shops and members of the family and I still have some. One thing I do not consider very helpful, in the long term, is to make the child's bedroom into a shrine, to the extent of never allowing anyone to touch anything. If they have toys and so on they should let other members of the family enjoy them, and just keep something, not everything back.

Through The Compassionate Friends' magazine I correspond with other parents who, like myself, have lost children abroad. Writing to them and meeting some of them has helped. I think I can say that, for us, the grieving time seemed to take longer as it was nearly two years to the day since Gary died before we attended the final inquest. It was like going back in time. Also, the driver's trial took place twenty months after we lost Gary. He was found guilty of dangerous driving and was banned for five years. I think I gradually came to realise that the driver did not intentionally cause the accident and, as my husband said, there, but for the grace of God, go I.

I received a letter from one of our old friends in Australia who said, 'Life goes on. You have another son and his wife and family and your husband. Don't let bitterness and hatred take over your life as in the end the only person you will destroy is yourself, and Gary would not like that. If Gary had a chance to live his life over again I know he would have chosen the same life.' I came to realise that what she said was true. Even my friends and relations and people at The Compassionate Friends saw a change in me. Sometimes in families, where a child has died, lots of other things seem to happen and you ask yourself why. Why me? Eight months after we lost Gary my husband lost his job in the City. This was a blow to us. He was fifty-four and did not have much chance of finding another job with the country in recession. He had so much time on his hands and periodically he would get depressed. I think men tend to keep their feelings bottled up, but the important thing is to try and talk about these things, and how you feel. We have been through some traumatic times, but you have to be strong for each other.

Since we lost Gary, there have been family weddings which sometimes are hard to get through; I find myself wondering, if he had lived, would he have been married now? Then there is the first of all your birthdays without them; the first anniversary of their death, no longer being able to say 'this time last year'; New Year's Eve with the song 'Auld Lang Syne' – these are all very difficult times. We had a new granddaughter born three years after Gary died, a little girl in the family at last, but at the same time we felt sad knowing Gary would not know her, or she him. Hearing a certain song on the radio, seeing people in the street that look like Gary, brings back all the feelings but somehow we overcome them. 'Life goes on'.

Speaking from experience, I think it is very important, especially when you lose a child abroad, to try and go back to where they died, as I had a picture in my mind and it was nothing like I imagined. We returned to Israel ten months after Gary died and for us the hardest part was to scatter his ashes. We went to Tiberius and scattered them near the Mount of Beatitudes. Israel was a place he loved and I felt like I was giving part of him back to the land. We stayed with his friends and now one thing I think is lovely is that his friends are now our friends and they visit us in England and we visit them in Israel. Every time we go to Israel we go to the scene of the accident and lay flowers on the wall. We visit the kibbutz from where Gary started out on that final day, the kibbutz where he and Susan first met. I always feel so close to Gary in Israel and have always said that I would return after my first holiday there. In some ways there were so many strange events that happened on our first visit to Israel and so many strange things that Gary said that I think he knew he was going to die. My husband and I both think there was a reason for his death and that he has gone to a better place, and that gives us comfort. Strange things have also happened since, and I know he is around us.

Not long after my husband was made redundant he spoke of moving, to clear our mortgage. I was quite horrified at first, as it would mean I would not be able to visit the crematorium every week, but I came to realise what my mother-in-law had told me – that your memories are not in bricks and mortar, they are inside you and you take them with you wherever you go. It was hard to even think about it, not being able to go to his bedroom – 'Gary's room' – any more. I know people who have moved too soon, thinking their grief will go away, and have then regretted it. You have to feel right about it. Anyway, fate took a hand when I was made redundant, so we had to move. Finally, five years after we lost our son, we moved from a thriving town to a very small, rural village. Life was strange at first, but now I really like it – bicycle-riding in the country, gardening, cooking, and so on. Lots of friends and family come to stay and when we go back to visit Stephen in Essex I try to go to the crematorium.

I really feel Gary would have approved of the life we are living now. I still write to his fiancée – it is nearly seven years on and she still calls us 'Mum' and 'Dad', which I think is lovely. She is a lovely young, attractive woman and I just hope she meets someone else one day and settles down to marry. She is back in her native Sweden and visits us occasionally. We will

never forget her and I know she will never forget Gary.
Something she told us when she came to England after Gary died
was that after he had taken us to the airport and returned to their
flat she asked him if it was hard for him to say goodbye to his
parents and he replied, 'It is always hard to say goodbye to people you love.' I will always treasure those words and his happy,
smiling face as he waved to us as we ascended the escalator. I
always called him 'Gary with the laughing eyes'.

So, for us, it will be seven years this year and I can honestly
say 'time is a great healer'. You will never forget the child you
have lost; a candle, a flame, will always burn to their memory.
There will be good and bad days; the bad days will be overcome.
There will be anger towards the people who avoid mentioning
your child's name or people who feel embarrassed when you
mention it, but you learn to get over this. We have some very
good friends who, on the anniversary of Gary's death and his
birthday, always send a card just to say 'Thinking of you'. Susan
also does this, which I think is beautiful. I always try very hard to
remember the happy times, full of sunshine and laughter – the
beautiful memories.

I know one day, Gary, I will see you again. 'Til the day we
meet again. Love, Mum and Dad.

Sylvia Wait

RACHEL

Our first child, Rachel, was born in July 1982. We had moved house the previous year in preparation for a family. My contract of work was completed and we looked forward eagerly to being parents. Although Rachel weighed over eight pounds at birth, as time went on she had some problems with feeding and her physical development failed to keep pace with that of her lively mind. When she was six weeks old, a heart murmur was detected and we were referred to a consultant paediatrician at the local hospital. The junior doctor, whom we saw first of all, said that everything seemed to be all right and I was not really surprised. Then the consultant came into the room, told us that in fact Rachel's condition was serious and that we would be referred to a consultant paediatric cardiologist at the regional hospital. Tears rolled down my cheeks on to Rachel who was cradled in my arms. We were given a cup of tea and went home to await our next appointment a few days later.

Our visit to the regional hospital confirmed that Rachel had a hole in her heart and problems with a valve. Although this was a terrible blow we hoped for successful surgery, perhaps by the time she was three years old. We did not realise until later the seriousness of her heart condition. Meanwhile, we tried to lead a normal family life. Rachel was very alert, gurgling happily and always watching the trees rather than sleeping when out in her pram. She seemed so full of life, often throwing her hands up in the air and when she was twelve weeks old she began to laugh. She did not look ill and, with her dark hair and without the chubby cheeks of a healthy baby, her face took on the refined and mature appearance of a much older child. She seemed to us to be a survivor and it was hard to imagine later that she must have been hanging on to life from the very beginning.

When she was four months old, Rachel was admitted to hospital, ostensibly to sort out her feeding problems. This proved to be an unhappy experience for both Rachel and me and on her fourth day in hospital she suddenly deteriorated and stopped breathing in her father's arms. She was resuscitated on the ward and rushed to intensive care while we waited anxiously for information in the company of the hospital chaplain. He baptised Rachel, barely recognisable under all the wires and tapes, as soon as we were admitted to her bedside.

For a week Rachel's life hung in the balance. We spent hours beside her bed during the day, hoping that she would know we were there, and would telephone the intensive care unit in the small hours to be told that she was stable. Life seemed to be a series of crises. On the Monday, Rachel was taken to another hospital for a brain scan and we were relieved to find that she had not suffered any brain damage as a result of her collapse. Emergency surgery was set to take place on Thursday afternoon, exactly one week after her collapse on the ward. On the Thursday morning we visited Rachel again; for the first time for a week, she was handed to me to hold, with all her wires attached, and I told her to make sure to come through the operation. I did not doubt, in fact, that she would do so.

At six o'clock we met the doctor who had looked after Rachel on the ward. We could see how difficult it was for her to tell us that it had been impossible to revive Rachel after the operation and we were grateful to the surgeon for suggesting a meeting at the end of a busy day to explain some of the detail of the operation. We drove home in the darkness feeling stunned, not yet having absorbed the realisation that we were no longer parents. We left the house again separately, almost immediately, to visit different friends and break the sad news. The restlessness of mind and body, which I felt that night and for which I was so unprepared, was to stay with me for a long time.

The extraordinary quiet in the house and the emptiness of Rachel's room in those dark November days were very hard to bear. The cot had been put up in readiness for her return home; we left this and all her belongings intact. Although her lively presence had gone, her room still held her inimitable baby smell and we felt no urgency to disturb things.

During the week between the operation and the funeral, people helped to sustain us. My mother-in-law, who had arrived on the day of the operation, helped to keep the house ticking over. Our neighbours, who had experienced the loss of children, provided us with wonderful take-away meals from their kitchen for the first two nights when normal, everyday tasks seemed monumentally difficult. Rachel's consultant paediatrician telephoned wanting to know the detail of what had happened. Our parish priest came to see us and, after listening to us talk about Rachel, said a prayer for her. He included so many aspects of her life and I wished that we could have recorded his words. On the Sunday the hospital chaplain conducted a short, intimate service for us as a family. We stood beside Rachel and felt close to her in a way which was not possible at the funeral. One of her grandmothers, who was to listen patiently to us as we worked through the events and asked ourselves unanswerable questions, and two friends who had been at our wedding came with us to the funeral. This was our third successive, terrible Thursday and for some time Thursdays assumed a very bleak significance in our lives. It was dark and raining in the mid-November afternoon, the crematorium seemed rather lofty and impersonal and the first thing that I noticed about the coffin, apart from its size, was that Rachel's name on the brass plate had been spelt incorrectly. We had chosen to have a private funeral, followed by cremation, but we had not considered the service in advance and I found it curiously inappropriate for a child.

As well as the obvious practical matters such as informing friends, some of whom lived far away and did not yet know of Rachel's birth, and making funeral arrangements, there were more trivial incidents that caused unnecessary distress and irritation. We had to register Rachel's death in a large, impersonal civic centre, queuing up with people who were waiting to register a birth. On visiting a dentist I had to persuade him that normal charges should not be levied since it was still within one year of our baby's birth, even if she was no longer with us. An embarrassing conversation through the grille at the post office led to correspondence with the head office in Glasgow as we tried to recoup savings that we had put into an account in Rachel's name. All these situations made us feel more isolated; what for us was a crushing tragedy seemed, to some people, to be no more than a matter of bureaucratic detail.

Somehow we existed through the nightmare of the next few weeks. The knowledge that we were no longer parents, at least in the eyes of the outside world, became a daily reality. Having continued to express milk for Rachel during the week between her collapse and the operation, the slow, sad, repetitive sound of the breast pump reminded us, day and night, of the physical loss. My check-up with a consultant gynaecologist, a man of realistic optimism and gentle humour, less than three weeks later, gave me the reassurance I needed to put me on the road to physical recovery. Quite soon after Rachel's death I knew deep down that the only way forward would be to try to become parents again. Knowing that I needed to be fit and as well as possible for this perhaps helped to prevent me from descending into a slough of despair. Some months afterwards we changed our GP, to one who was more understanding and talked about Rachel quite naturally, and this too was helpful.

At home, we talked endlessly about Rachel to each other, to our mothers and those closest to us trying to recall everything she had done in her 116 days. We imitated her mannerisms and interpreted them in words just as we had done when she was alive. We liked talking about her because we loved her. Her bouncing chair and two favourite toys remained downstairs with us and at first it was not unusual to feel her presence and that she was still sitting there following us with her eyes. Sometimes the memories made us laugh but quite often we cried, sometimes loudly in acute anguish, sometimes softly in near despair. These powerfully turbulent feelings gradually gave way to calmer waters although new or unexpected circumstances would provoke an anguished response months, or even years, later.

As well as the constant struggle to come to terms with what had happened to us, two memories in particular stand out from the early weeks. I planted bulbs in the garden in the hope that we would feel better by the time the flowers emerged from the ground. We had one session of genetic counselling, which left me feeling that we might never have a family. The advice was found later to have been based on a case which had no relevance to ours. However, I was determined not to go under; we had, after all, had a daughter who had been happy and I knew that she would not have wanted her parents to be unhappy. Although I had loved and lost, I did not stop loving Rachel or my husband who had to go on with his job, teaching students, as though nothing had happened.

We felt very strongly that there were some general lessons to be learned about the care of children in hospital as a result of Rachel's time as an in-patient before her collapse. We thought carefully through the experience as a whole and discussed with each other in detail what we should write. Before our six-week follow-up meeting with Rachel's consultant paediatric cardiologist we submitted four pages of observations to him. Although we realised that our remarks would seem subjective, we wrote in our covering letter that we did not feel anger or hostility towards anyone concerned with Rachel's care. We did, however, feel that unnecessary distress had been caused to her through the administration of hospital procedures, sometimes without warning and often in our absence. The shortage of skilled nursing staff and the failure to improve on the feeding regime which had already been established at home, coupled with the strained atmosphere caused by a strike of ancillary workers, had all undermined my confidence in the purpose of Rachel's stay in hospital and my place as a resident parent. It was beneficial to be able to voice our disquiet and some of our suggestions were implemented subsequently.

My lingering wish that I had not left Rachel alone in the hospital for what proved to be her last night of normality, living without the aid of a ventilator and my regret that I was not there to feed her when she woke, as she must have done, were counterbalanced by the knowledge that my exhaustion, as a result of hospital routine and lack of sleep, was at the time overwhelming and drove me to seek a relatively peaceful night at home. We shall never know if her catastrophic decline overnight and collapse the following day were inevitable but we do know that Rachel's clinical condition was far worse than it was possible to assess before her operation. The comforting words of a friend who said to me that we can only do what seems best at the time have remained with me.

In order to escape the festivities and duties of Christmas at home, and to seek some anonymity, we planned to spend Christmas in Paris borrowing a friend's flat for two weeks. As we were transported across France by coach, in thick fog, the change of surroundings began to have a beneficial effect. We walked along quiet streets to Notre Dame on Christmas morning, sat talking in pavement cafés and began to look to the future again. The entries in my diary, which had remained blank since late October while I recorded things simply on the family calendar, came to life again in late December. There were trips to the Louvre, to Delacroix's house and studio, the Jardin des Plantes, Montmartre and the elegant St Germain-en-Laye as we revisited some well loved familiar haunts and discovered some new ones. I tried to describe in my diary the paintings we saw and even the meals we cooked in the tiny kitchen. I made lists of things to be done in the house in the new year. It was good for us to have precious time together away from the pressures of work and the demands of everyday life at home.

On our return I began to decorate the house, enrolled for classes in art and gardening and bought a second-hand bicycle. All this helped to divert my mind and assuage some of my restlessness. The art classes took place one morning each week in a market town a half hour's drive from home. The distance from home was important and the art centre provided unfamiliar surroundings in which I could be completely absorbed while experimenting with different media. I began to grow plants from seed and have found this a fascinating and exciting pastime ever since; in fact I am sure that my developing love of the garden and tending plants has been one of the most relaxing and therapeutic occupations I have discovered in the last ten years.

Three months after Rachel died, the photographs we had taken of her were developed. Perhaps I had delayed this because I felt that to see her face again might be too painful to bear. However, I was so thrilled when I collected them that I rushed straight round to show them to an old friend who had known Rachel and loved her. The photographs of Rachel, looking so happy and full of life, became a great source of solace and joy and sometimes helped to break the ice in conversation with friends and colleagues. Years later they continue to bring happiness and revive good memories along with all the other family photographs dotted around the house and in my husband's office.

A colleague from my previous job invited me to do a few days' work, travelling around schools and interviewing teachers. Before Easter I took the plunge and began to apply for other jobs. In April I started a part-time job in a library where the work was fairly easy and helped to restore some of my lost confidence. It was difficult to accept the fact that I was going back to work because if Rachel had been alive, I would not have been doing so. However, I got used to the routine and a few weeks later we went to a party for which I made a new dress. I had looked forward to sewing for my daughter and found myself unable to contemplate dress-making after she died. We enjoyed ourselves at the party and this seemed to be quite a step forward. We had both made a conscious decision not to wear sombre colours; the greys and browns in our wardrobe gave way to reds and blues which we have worn ever since.

On Rachel's first birthday I received beautiful flowers from my husband and his mother and, from friends, a lovely posy of deep pink carnations and *alchemilla mollis* which so reminded me of Rachel that I wrote in my diary 'very bright and cheerful like little Poppet'. I howled tears of anguish at the end of that hot, sunny Sunday but it was the first of many staging posts and we have tried, since then, to celebrate the occasion with a family outing and a picnic.

Friends in other parts of the country offered us places to stay for short holidays and we gradually began to feel better. We went out, met friends and life resumed a kind of normality, albeit superficially since we knew that we had suffered a loss that could never be put completely behind us. That summer I grew some colourful coleus plants from seed, festooned the garden with hanging baskets and felt the warm sunny weather heal some of the wounds.

In the autumn we decided to do a first-aid course together. I was pregnant again and wanted to be able to cope with any emergency with a new baby. This was hard for my husband as he feels naturally queasy under these circumstances but we persevered, passed our examination and became absorbed with the familiar nest building that accompanies a pregnancy. This time, as we put up shelves, decorated and improved the practical layout in Rachel's room we knew how little time there would be for such things after the birth.

Instead of returning to the local hospital where Rachel had been born, I opted to attend the ante-natal clinic at a specialist maternity hospital. It was further from home and entailed more travelling but I wanted to be in the care of the consultant whom I had seen shortly after Rachel's death. During the next few months I was really grateful to him, and to everyone at the hospital, for providing such relaxed surroundings in which I could feel

like an ordinary expectant mother. I wanted everything to pro-
ceed naturally and mercifully it did. We decided against amnio-
centesis; in fact, I did not give it much consideration as I did not
want to take any unnecessary risks on behalf of the baby. Also,
my long-held belief that I could not willingly have agreed to a
termination was sharply reinforced by the knowledge that,
despite all the agony and worry we had experienced, Rachel's
life had brought us such joy.

Just before Christmas our second baby's heart was scanned in
the womb by Rachel's consultant cardiologist. The news that all
seemed to be well gave us the Christmas present we had hoped
for and we spent Christmas peacefully at home. After the scan
we felt optimistic and more relaxed and I continued to work part-
time until my temporary post came to an end. I enjoyed the rest
of the time before the birth and did not feel too apprehensive
about the outcome. I felt calm and hopeful that it would turn out
well and, as I got up in the small hours to read or sew, I knew that
we had a vigourous member of the family on board.

On Easter Sunday we had lunch with the friends and neighbours who had looked after us so well immediately after Rachel
died. Easter was late and we sat in the garden in warm spring
sunshine. On the Tuesday evening we went for a walk as usual
and a few hours later found ourselves driving, unhindered by any
traffic, towards the hospital. A fine healthy boy was born and I
felt so contented and so happy as I lay looking at him on that first
day. He was his own person right from the beginning and I loved
him unreservedly as I had loved Rachel. Her paediatrician, who
had kept in touch with us, and had insisted that I telephone him
when I went into labour, even if this was in the middle of the
night, arranged for one of his colleagues to examine our baby
within hours of his birth. We left for home two days later to start
our family life for the second time.

Friends, and even people we hardly knew, joined in the celebration of this new life as we settled down to satisfy the hunger
and curiosity for living which our son brought with him. It did

seem that this new focus allowed people to relate more naturally towards us again. This time the heart murmur detected in the early weeks, turned out to be one of those that occur in a third of all babies. Knowing that our son was perfectly healthy has made everything seem more natural and seeing him progress through the different stages of childhood has been the very best of therapies. We felt a sense of freedom, seeing his robustness and obvious good health, in giving him scope to explore his world to the full. At the same time, our increased knowledge of childhood illnesses and sudden accidents made us more aware of that fine balance of life which exists especially in the first year. During the first two years we had regular appointments, first of all with Rachel's paediatric cardiologist and then her consultant paediatrician, which helped to reassure us that our son was as well as he appeared to be. Our health visitor also called to see us regularly and became a family friend.

Having been deprived of Rachel's company at such an early stage in my relationship with her I was determined to be fully involved in the early years of our son's life. We had a busy time, making friends, visiting toddler groups, swimming and doing all the things that make up the pre-school life of an energetic child. I wanted to give him the benefit of my earlier experience of teaching young children and the house quickly became a hive of creative activity. I felt myself coming to life again and often felt tremendous joy on seeing this young life flourishing alongside all the other children whom we got to know. Perhaps our delight in witnessing this progress and our appreciation of our son as a person have been heightened by the previous tragedy. Certainly, there is an awareness that personal happiness can be overturned in a moment and that everyday experiences are valuable and to be cherished. Occasionally, during the pre-school years, when in the company of small children, I could become acutely aware of my own loss but this eased when school took the place of playgroup and there were more opportunities for adult-based activities.

I went to history classes and then, the following year, to language classes in preparation for a three-month family trip to Europe in connection with my husband's work. This journey across Europe, living in different countries for short periods and our shared experiences strengthened the bonds that we feel as a small family. We had an exciting time travelling through France, Belgium and Germany, staying in Berlin just before the Wall came down. Our son went to school just outside Paris for a month and we joined in the *Bicentenaire* festivities to celebrate two hundred years of the French Republic. We returned to this country feeling stimulated and renewed by our experiences.

I had been working part-time from home since our son went to playgroup when he was two and a half. Eventually, when he was six I found another job which was challenging and demanding. It had been newly created and turned out to be more time-consuming than I had supposed initially. For a time life constantly required extra organisation, especially as my mother became ill 250 miles away and I tried to balance the demands of the job with the needs of the immediate and extended family. With the support of my husband, and a wonderful band of student helpers, I was relieved to find that I could cope with a life that would have seemed impossible seven years previously. Eight years after Rachel's death, we celebrated Christmas with my brother and his family who were visiting us from Australia. As I had not seen my brother for eighteen years, nor previously met his children, this was a tremendous occasion and we had a wonderful week together.

Undoubtedly, there are some times of the year that seem more difficult than others, although quite often the anticipation of a particular day or event has turned out to be worse than the reality. The anniversary of Rachel's death, in early November, is one such time although by the first anniversary we were looking forward to another birth and in the years that followed, we had the demands of a young child to divert us. Remembrance Sunday occasionally falls on or near the anniversary of Rachel's funeral and this too reminds us of those gloomy, dark days. For her birthday or anniversary I have often arranged for a mass to be said in her memory. Three years ago a book of remembrance was started at the hospital where she died and the name of each child is recorded on the appropriate day. There is some solace in seeing Rachel's full name written in beautiful script and a visit to the chapel, where the book has been placed, gives me a focus for the day. On the tenth anniversary of her death I took a bunch of pink carnations to the children's ward and, another year, bought a lamp to symbolise the light and joy that Rachel brought into our lives. The fact that those few people who were at the funeral with us also remember her anniversary means a great deal to us.

However, it is not just the anniversaries which may be hard to get through; as time goes on these can, in a sense, be prepared for. It is the unexpected which sometimes brings tears to the eyes and highlights the emotional vulnerability. Sometimes, a return to a familiar place for a holiday can be a trigger for sadness, either soon after bereavement or even at a later stage. We returned to a cottage, for a holiday, some months after Rachel died and exactly a year after our previous visit. I found then that there were too many memories of our earlier, happier times there but many subsequent visits to the same cottage have been happy and beneficial.

Even ten years later, on returning to Norfolk, whilst looking at pictures in a gallery where we had bought our first painting together, the memories of carefree holidays enjoyed there before we had a family came flooding back. I was quite suddenly struck by the magnitude of what had happened to us since we had last been there and I found myself incongruously and uncontrollably engulfed by tears. It was a beautiful, sunny day and I was taken completely by surprise. I have learned to accept this vulnerability as part of my being and not to be ashamed of it. At other times, I can feel stronger and enjoy life in a way that I could not have foreseen in the aftermath of Rachel's death.

Apart from Rachel's paediatrician and his family who have

been a tremendous support to us throughout the last twelve years, including us in their family life when we had lost ours, and the humane and humorous GP to whom we later changed, the medical profession seemed strangely at a loss in offering us any help in the early stages. However helpful professional theories about bereavement may be to those seeking to help, the greatest support may come from someone simply being there, listening and taking an interest and not being afraid to ask about the child who has died. A simple message, some flowers, an acknowledgment in the street are all relevant and remembered for a very long time afterwards. Refraining from using the child's name or, as time elapses, failing to acknowledge that anything important has happened to the bereaved parents keeps the sadness locked inside and makes these negative reactions hard to bear.

It takes time, of course, to listen to another's story and it can be painful for friends and family to see someone they love in such distress. Self-help may, in some circumstances, be the only source of aid. My own search for a calmer mind and body led me, after some years, to a relaxation method that takes the muscles from a state of tension to one of ease in a relatively short time. This helps to counteract the inability to relax which I found was one of the worst aspects of bereavement. A book and a tape explain the process simply and it can be covered in about half an hour if one is fairly sure of being undisturbed; or it can lead to a longer period of rest and sleep if time allows.

Whilst suffering some neck and shoulder problems, I tried other relaxation methods, including yoga, and also had sessions of osteopathy but found the Mitchell method[4] to be the most beneficial in the long term. My correspondence with the author was a tremendous consolation at a time when conventional treatment was not proving successful. I have continued to practise her method and find it a wonderful oasis in a busy schedule. Some homeopathic and herbal remedies have also been helpful in inducing better sleep and a more tranquil approach to life.

Another aspect of grief was that although I loved reading, I could not, for some time after Rachel died, bring myself to read anything that described family life. Months later, a friend gave me a copy of a book by a well-known author[5] which recounted the life and tragic early death of her grown-up daughter. I could not share her belief in mystical experiences but I found the story fascinating and realised that I could again be engrossed in reading. A number of authors, well-known writers in other genres, have written about their own experience of losing a child; reading these accounts, full of passion and strength, of ordeals different from mine and yet having some elements in common, has broadened my perspective on my own loss.

As our son was born after Rachel's death, it is difficult for him to relate to her as a person but we have gradually told him more about her life and death as he has become more able to understand it. He played with her toys and is used to seeing photographs of her among the other family mementos. Over the years we have not hidden our feelings about Rachel and a warm hug from him on her tenth birthday helped to stem the flow of my tears. We always light a candle for Rachel when visiting a church and recently, when walking around the village graveyard near our home, we explained that she had been cremated because we had not wanted to think of her lying in the cold ground. It is important to us that he knows about Rachel's life and knows how we feel about her.

Since our bereavement, over ten years ago, a growing public awareness of the effects of loss has led to more open discussion, particularly in the media, and opportunities for counselling, drop-in sessions and help in general for people suffering this state of being. Having read some of the literature describing the 'stages of bereavement', I am not aware that our recovery followed any particular pattern. We did not conform to the frequently quoted stages of anger and guilt as we felt, when we looked back over Rachel's life, that we had made the most of our time with her and done everything for her that we possibly could.

It was the feeling of overwhelming, dulling sadness which

dominated the early months and which has recurred occasionally since then; the realisation that this lovely little person, who had so quickly become the centre of our love, could so quickly vanish and leave an enormous chasm in our everyday life and in our future. We had for years looked forward to being parents and overnight that joy had been taken from us. I had known the strength of my own feeling for Rachel and witnessed the strong bond between father and daughter; he was so gentle and patient, so delighted to be her father and so good at it. We had been, briefly, *so happy* and the wrench was terrible. The future seemed a void. We felt that our lives had come to an end and I vividly remember in my mind a blackness which I can only describe as a tunnel.

The repercussions of such a deep loss may last a lifetime but the laughter and fun can return. We see each day as precious and there is an extra dimension in our life which brings both strength and vulnerability. Our experience has given us more confidence in dealing with other situations and an ability to cope with disaster whilst at the same time leaving us less able to contemplate doing so. Despite all the pain and sadness, we do feel fortunate in the way that both our children have played their part in enriching our being and opening our eyes to so many things.

Katherine Woodward

SAMANTHA

April 22nd 1989. It should have been the beginning of summer. Instead, it was the beginning of the rest of our lives and the end of Samantha's.

After a day at school and four hours working in the local supermarket, Sam and Catherine, her lifelong friend, put on their glad rags and joyously rushed off into the night. Both girls were extremely happy; 'A' Level studies were exciting and challenging and they had money to spend after working in the supermarket for two evenings a week. Catherine supplemented this by waitressing and Sam babysat and acted as a summer lifeguard. Their lives lay tantalisingly ahead of them in journalism for Catherine and teaching for Sam.

As usual I knew I wouldn't settle until the girls arrived home. Nick, our son, came and talked in our bedroom before going to bed himself, telling us of his evening out with his friends and planning tomorrow's events. Nick was nineteen and Sam seventeen. They were both in Belper School's sixth form.

Now for the wait for the girls – wait, wait, wait. I dozed and then woke with a start. I looked at the clock – 1.45 a.m. They were late! As time slowly passed panic increased. I checked Sam's room, but of course the beds, amidst the chaos of discarded supermarket uniform and make-up, were empty. Eventually I woke John, my husband, who had tried to ignore my earlier pacing. Something had to be done. I decided to phone Stephen, Sam's man of the moment, as he had taken them out in his mother's car.

I had never looked in Sam's Filofax before, but something had to be done. I felt so guilty for phoning so late. Stephen's father answered, his voice echoing confusion. The ringing telephone, the simultaneous knock on the door. I'd no sooner said I was Sam's mother when another male voice, most definitely that of a police officer, came on the line asking who I was and was my husband with me. Time froze. John, fully awake by this time, grabbed the bedside telephone. 'Yes, my daughter is Samantha Morris. An accident. Is she dead?' asked John, as he knew his wise and sensible daughter would have contacted us if at all possible. 'Yes,' said the distressed officer. 'We will be with you as soon as possible.' The phone went dead.

No, no, no. Utter disbelief. The air was sucked from my lungs. How can this be true? Comprehension escaped us. Did we cry? I am not sure; we must have done as Nick woke to the nightmare. He told me he woke to the sound of me noisily hyperventilating and gasping for breath. I remember little of that. We three clung to each other. In a total haze we dressed. I do remember thinking 'what should I wear?' as Sam had such good dress sense. What do you wear for this?

Two police officers soon arrived, one male, one female. There were tears and absolute disbelief. I remember the lady officer taking Nick into the kitchen to make the first of the incalculable number of cups of tea. They had told us that Sam was dead, but it never occurred to me that Catherine wasn't dead. Sadly, they confirmed that she too was dead.

We were told that both girls had died instantly, on impact. Stephen, the driver, was in hospital, badly injured, but at that time thought not to be critical. His family had gone to him. (Stephen did in fact survive after much surgery and many weeks in hospital.) The police told us there was another injured passenger, but who was he? Samantha, Catherine and Stephen had gone out together, but we had no idea who had joined them. This young man was alive but very badly injured, and he had been transferred to the neurosurgical unit in Nottingham. Later that day he was identified as Simon but sadly he died the following day. Judy, a close friend of Samantha, had gone to the United

States on a school exchange and Simon was her boyfriend. What a homecoming awaited her three days later.

Probably because everything is so unreal your mind is incapable of true comprehension. You don't feel it's actually happening to you; it's rather as if you are acting out the scene on a stage and everyone is just a player. Any minute you will wake from this nightmare.

Catherine was an only child. Jean, her mother, had married Paddy three weeks earlier. Cath had been so happy. This could not be happening to our families. We had already experienced such similar tragedies. Catherine's seventeen-year-old cousin, Alan, had been killed in a road traffic accident two and a half years earlier and John's sister, Rosalind (Sam's aunt), had been killed in a road traffic accident in 1960. She too was seventeen. How could it happen again?

We met outside the Accident and Emergency Department at the Derbyshire Royal Infirmary. Totally numb, Jean and I clung to each other and wept. I remember her saying, 'Our beautiful girls. Our beautiful girls.'

We were taken to a small, dreary room, full of an assortment of chairs and people. More tea arrived. I don't remember anyone drinking it. The police officers sat with us, as did two or three nurses. Amidst all this horror strange practical thoughts jumped into my mind. They were probably trying to block out the horror of it all. John had injured a knee three weeks earlier, while skiing. I remember asking the nurse to cancel his next appointment with the casualty consultant. I also recall telling the sister I remembered her as a student nurse on Community Placement. Totally insane, and such trivia. Thinking back, we were all terribly restrained; we were in 'shock' I suppose. We could not fully comprehend what had happened.

Both Jean and John expressed concern for their respective parents. These grandparents had suffered before. How would they cope? Both grandfathers were frail. This horror was bound to harm them still more. We were told that, for legal purposes, the

girls must be officially identified. The hospital staff described the
girls, but initially they needed to establish who was who. They
had been carrying very little in the way of identification themselves, just one handbag and one purse between them. The handbag was Cath's, the purse Sam's.

When John's father had identified Rosalind in 1960 it had been
routine for the father to identify his child. I had occasionally
thought about it and felt in a vague 'it will never happen to us'
sort of way that, as parents, we would be together. Nick was
asked if he wished to come with us too, but he was adamant that
he did not wish to see Sam. I felt it right that he had the opportunity; there would be time later if he changed his mind. He didn't
as it happened, and so far he does not regret the decision.

To identify your dead child is terrifying. As a nurse I have
cared for the dead many times; I had been with both my parents
at their deaths, but this was different. Nothing can prepare you to
see your own child – I was terrified. How did John feel? How did
Jean and Paddy feel? They had not seen anyone dead before. It
occurred to me even in that dreary little room, before we were
taken to the mortuary, that if I was terrified, how must they be
feeling?

Many images remain. The mortuary is one. Faces were
blurred, voices muted. Clinging on to each other, we looked
down at Sam's lovely face. Very peaceful; very quiet. There was
a slight bruise on her temple and her front teeth were smashed;
otherwise she could have been asleep. Those moments are etched
on your memory for the rest of your life. Dare we touch her?
Nobody said. We kissed her, sobbed, stroked her face, but we
were afraid to touch her more because of the illogical idea that if
we did we might hurt her. We had been told that she had died of a
broken neck (despite seat belt and head restraint) but she must,
we felt, have more injuries. No one told us she was otherwise
uninjured. Her lovely, lithe young body was hidden from us not
only by the sheet, but by our fear and uncertainty. I remember
nothing of leaving the mortuary.

Grandparents had to be told. I remember thinking that my parents did not have to endure this as they too were dead. For once I felt grateful for this. After stopping at John's parents' home I travelled to our home in Belper in the police car. Nick sat up in front with the driver as he had done on the journey in. John stayed with his parents, helped them dress and organise themselves before being driven to our home by a friend. Sitting in the large police car, which felt like a capsule in outer space, I lost all track of time. I wondered why people were rushing around, oblivious, shopping, filling the car with petrol. How stupid they were because time and life had stopped.

Nick and I let ourselves in to a still and empty house. We half expected Sam to come downstairs and demand to know where we had been. John and his parents arrived. The five of us sat and waited. What for we hadn't a clue. The GP arrived, sat in an upright chair and hid behind his case. We said we didn't want any medication. He said 'Good' and left. Friends arrived; who and for how long I have no idea. Periods of numbness and inertia were interspersed with frantic activity. Adrenalin pumped; so much to do. Phone calls to be made, people to tell. Then total inertia again. Food was prepared but was largely ignored.

During the afternoon I watched Nick through the window. He wore his cherished long black coat which he and Sam had found in a second-hand shop. He was now calling on friends, telling them the awful news. My active, bemused son needed something to do. This terrible day passed. We all went to bed, but no one knew if they would sleep. Nick brought his sleeping bag and lay down beside us. He fell asleep holding John's hand. We slept downstairs as John's parents had our room. We couldn't sleep in Sam's room at that time, but right from the beginning we used it. Amidst the chaos of a teenage girl's room Nick sat and talked to their friends and each day, up to the funeral, after the hundreds of cards and letters were delivered, we sat as a family in Sam's room and tried to read them. It felt right to be there.

It's a very frightening experience to anyone, of whatever age, to visit the bereaved, and when you are a teenager it is not what you expect to be doing, but these beautiful young people came – and they still come. Their love for our daughter and their love and care for us have supported and cherished us since that dreadful day. They came and gave us their hearts. Their letters, cards and poems are wonderful and precious. They shared with us their lives with Samantha. As a close family we thought we knew Sam, but they showed us another Sam, one whom we feel very privileged to know.

We have had so much love and support from friends and family and to them I give my heartfelt thanks, but I do want to tell more of our wonderful young people in Belper. Belper is a small market town with a population of about 15,000. Both Sam and Cath were born and brought up in the town. They had gone through school together. They were well known and popular.

Monday morning arrived; just another week to the rest of the world. Close friends had been with Nick on Saturday and Sunday, but school had to be faced. Louise, Sam's friend who was two weeks younger than Sam and lived next door, drove up to school with Nick. They walked into a quiet school and on to a silent sixth-form common room. Sixth-form common rooms filled with young people are never quiet, but this one was. Normally music blared, laughter abounded. This was a happy school. These were bright, happy and secure young people. There was silence. Teenagers with white, strained faces sprawled on chairs and sat on the floor. Nick eventually spoke, I am told. What he said I don't know, but they told me his words gave them permission to talk, to ask questions and to cry. Yes, they cried; boys and girls, students and staff.

By the time Nick came home to a bulging house, plans were being made. We had already decided to have a joint funeral. It was too much to expect their friends, and everyone else, to attend two funerals, and we felt it right to join together in this. It was a very good decision. Sixth-form classes were suspended for the week. No one, staff or students, could have worked. However, they were busy. They were busy loving us, staying with us singly, and in groups. Nick brought us plans from school. He told us that he and some of the boys who were particularly friendly with both Sam and Cath wished to carry their coffins. Jason, Nick's friend, had asked if he could play the organ at the service. At that time we were unaware that Jason had ever played a church organ before!

Nick's greatest help at this time came from a young friend called Rachel who lived in Nottingham. Nick and Sam's friendship with her had begun four years previously on our first skiing holiday, and although their only contact had been on the annual ski trips, plus an occasional party or concert visit, they developed a deep and caring friendship. At the time of Sam's death Rachel was doing voluntary work after 'A' Levels before taking up her studies as a medical student. She quickly came to Nick's side, and ours too. She was with us throughout the following week. This was in direct contrast to Nick's cousins. They had been very close throughout their childhood and at one period the girls had lived with us. The eldest cousin, who is six months older than Nick, was at this time a second-year medical student, and she found it impossible to relate to him. In fact she said, 'People expect that I can help Nick and yet I find it impossible.'

Gradually all the plans began to evolve into a celebration of Samantha's and Catherine's lives. The service was to be in our local parish church, followed by cremation. How do you choose whether to bury or cremate your child? Jean's preference was for cremation, and this was right for us too. Jean and Paddy and John and I met together as much as possible to arrange this celebration of our daughters' lives. Finding quiet moments to talk and plan was hard. So many people came to see us and to share our grief, but we had to make time for ourselves. We didn't want a morbid funeral and, with the help of an understanding vicar and friends in the church, we arranged a memorable and beautiful service.

On the evening before the funeral John and I went down to the church. Nick was already there. Jason was being instructed by the church organist on the intricacies of the organ. We walked in to the sounds of 'Yesterday'. The ladies of the church were putting the finishing touches to the flower arrangements. No bride could have entered a more beautifully decorated church; yellow and blue spring flowers were everywhere. Flowers on the altar, adorning the screen, the pews and on every available ledge. With the beauty of the music and the flowers we could feel the love and support surrounding us.

Friday eventually arrived. The funeral was scheduled for one o'clock, but the sixth form had arranged their own memorial service in the main school hall at nine o'clock. Although we had seen so many of their friends during the week, actually entering school, the girls' territory, was daunting. We went into a silent hall. At the front a low table filled with flowers and an enlarged photograph of the girls faced us. To the right, four young men with guitars and drums waited to play. The service that followed was both beautiful and moving. Poems were read, pop music played, and young people bravely and tearfully spoke of Sam and Cath. After this service we moved to the front of the school for a tree-planting ceremony. In a way this was a little light relief. Two trees had been purchased, ground was prepared and a brass plaque erected, yet to be unveiled by Nick. Bouquets of flowers, single red roses with messages, covered the ground.

Tim and Paul, two close friends of the girls, spoke on behalf of the school. They spoke of not losing friends, but sisters. They spoke of their love for them. While we listened we were surrounded by staff, students and even the dinner ladies who often gave Sam their healthy-eating recipes.

Two trees, one a crab apple and one a flowering cherry, lay ready to be planted. Louise was to plant one and another friend, Joanne, would plant the other. Their efforts were to be applauded, but John smilingly suggested he give them gardening lessons. Left to their planting skills, the trees would not be blooming as they are today. After Nick unveiled the plaque we had coffee with their closest friends and some of the staff, then we reluctantly returned home. The thought of following our daughter's coffin was too horrendous to contemplate, but having seen her in the chapel of rest I knew that the body was not my daughter, but was there to represent her. Samantha was wherever we believed her to be in the next life. It was that belief which saw us through. We slowly travelled the half-mile to church. Groups of people stood outside houses, on street corners and the cobbled areas in front of the church. Nick joined the eleven other young men who stood waiting to receive their burdens. There they stood – in smart suits, black ties and white shirts. Would Sam and Cath recognise them?

The sky was blue. It was a beautiful April day. Tearful, friendly, caring faces embraced us as we followed the girls down the church path. The beautifully decorated church was full to overflowing, but to us it was a sea of faces. We often talk of that service with pleasure. It was as we had planned. The emotion and love could be felt. The hymns 'Love Divine' and 'All Things Bright and Beautiful' were perfect. The address was given by the girls' history and form tutor, John March, whom they both loved dearly. His words were wonderful and he captured the girls' personalities to the letter. When he finished there was utter silence. I have heard that one young man had said he had wanted to clap. I wish he had. It would have felt so right.

We passed through the town on the way to the crematorium. Again, groups of people stood in quiet respect. In ones, twos and more. We were so pleased to share this celebration of Sam's life with so many people. Many came to the house; some obviously found it harder than others. Sam's uncle and godfather (John's brother), who lives in Canada, decided not to come as he apparently felt his distress would upset us. John later explained to him how we could not have been more distressed and by sharing our loss with those who cared we gained strength to carry on. We have many cameo memories of those hours. One is of the lovely, gentle vicar arriving on his bicycle, complete with wicker basket on the handlebars. Decked out in clerical collar and cycle clips he joined our celebration by enjoying a number of large whiskies. Our great concern was his safety on his journey home down the long, steep hill on to the busy A6.

Some days after the funeral Nick came to see us and told us that he and a group of friends would like to record a tape in memory of Sam and Cath in the newly opened recording studio in the school. This proved to be both therapeutic and pleasurable. Soon after Sam's death Nick had found an anonymous poem called 'Present in Absence'. This poem beautifully described how, although absent, one is still present in the mind. The words were arranged and music composed for the title song on the tape. By arranging this, organising suitable songs and deciding who should sing them, their friends were able to express their feelings for Sam and Cath in a way that is fundamentally important to young people – music. The result of their labours staggered and amazed us all in the emotion and skill displayed.

This tape was recorded and a professional cover was produced, again by the students themselves. They raised £2000 – £1000 went to the Derbyshire Royal Infirmary Flying Squad, who cared for the girls at the scene of the accident, and £1000 was given to the school.

We are now five years on. John and I miss and love Sam as much today as the day she died. Dealing with the changes within the family is always difficult, but when your child dies difficulties increase as many beliefs are challenged. However close parents are they grieve for their child in different ways. Not that one loves the child more than they do each other, but each relationship with that child is unique. We are fortunate as our grieving was not significantly different. We both cried openly, talked openly, and both of us were happy to be surrounded by photographs of Sam's lovely face. We cherish every moment we had with our daughter, but we have survived five years and have slowly found that life can go on, and happily at times. At the beginning you are frightened of losing your child altogether, but you don't. In some way they are closer, deep within your heart.

At every celebration, be it Christmas, birthdays, anniversaries, graduations or weddings, Sam will not physically be there, but she is there in our hearts. We cope at these times by talking of her. We learn to miss her; to help ourselves through these celebratory times a change in routine eases the hurt. This could be by changing the way you spend Christmas Day or simply where you display the birthday card. As a family we have always been surrounded by the children's photographs, so it was natural for us to continue. In the early days I became frantic about finding photographs. You can always tell a bereaved parent at the photography counter by his or her paranoia over the print or the negative. The poor assistant is lectured severely on the need for care.

Slowly we began to sort out Sam's room. It is still, and always will be, known as Sam's room, but it has changed in subtle ways, although it has not been redecorated as Sam, with Dad's help, had decorated it only weeks before she died. Special clothes, jewellery and books were given to close friends. It has all been done at our pace, no one else's. We are down to two drawers crammed with very special clothing, jewellery and Sam's significant bits and bobs. We still have her flute and her 'A' Level work-books. One day there may be the right person to have her flute. I sometimes wear her clothes; I'm sure she wouldn't mind as I regularly wore her cast offs! I sometimes even sleep in her bed when we have visitors, and I do enjoy that. Her room is very much part of the house.

As far as guilt and anger are concerned we, as many parents do initially, feel guilty at being alive and angry not only at what happened, but at life itself. I felt I had no right to happiness. I felt the physical pain of Sam's death and wanted to hold on to it because that made her still real. This pain does ease and you learn to live again. All the assumptions in my life had to be reassessed and gradually the pain eased. I feel I have now internalised Sam in my heart – not that pain never returns; it does, sometimes suddenly, often at significant occasions such as Christmas, her birthday or the date of her death – but I know now that the pain will go and Sam is safe in my heart.

As I mentioned before, John's sister, Rosalind, died aged seventeen and now his seventeen-year-old daughter has died too. He still loves and misses his sister, but does say the loss cannot be compared for him to the death of his daughter. Since Sam's death he has learned how his parents coped. As an active fifteen-year-old he immersed himself in his sport. He felt responsible for his younger brother and sister, but did not see his parents' desolation. When John first told me about Rosalind he said he felt guilty at refusing to go to the cinema with her the weekend before she died and then, after Sam died, he wondered if he was the catalyst. These thoughts were all bound up in natural feelings of guilt at still being alive. Of course, he knew, and now accepts, that he was not responsible. In a way, it seems that the loss of Samantha has brought Rosalind more alive.

Nick once said that he wasn't meant to be an only child. He now realises he is not an only child as Sam remains very much his loving, steadfast and bossy sister. He is still happy not to have seen her after she died, remembering her as she was. We found it easy to talk of her and still do to anyone who will listen. Some people never mention her, but others that do are my 'special people'. I am told that others do remember, but how I wish they would say so. I think a parent's greatest fear is that their child will be forgotten.

I used to hate the phrase 'time heals'. I thought if I heal Sam will be gone. I know now that this is not true. It is just like a scar – always there. Like the scar on my right hand the scar of Samantha's death is on my heart and soul and as my hand works, so do my heart and soul; changed, but still working. It takes time really to live again and to be positive about life, and it was perhaps about three years before I could see and feel the beauty in our world. John appreciated it far sooner than I did but one morning, while driving to work, I suddenly saw and felt the beauty of the valley around me.

We had been able to mark Samantha's eighteenth birthday by the presentation of the £1000 cheque to the Flying Squad. Her twenty-first birthday fell on a Saturday and we wanted to celebrate and mark the occasion, so we invited special friends to come and share in a celebration of her birth and her life. We made no secret of why we were getting together. Being surrounded by loving and caring people, who Samantha still means something to, carried us through what could have been a very desolate time.

Looking back at that terrible day in 1989 I am very pleased that the sister in the Accident and Emergency Department wrote on the plain brown envelope containing the 'sudden death' information the telephone number of the local branch of The Compassionate Friends. At the time my fog-filled mind read it and discarded it. The days following the funeral were painful and lonely, and at one particularly devastating moment I felt we could not get through alone. I picked up the telephone and dialled the number and, at the other end, I heard the caring voice of our County Contact for the Compassionate Friends. It was the beginning of the rest of my life. Even with the wonderful community support, a loving family and two other families intimately involved sharing our loss, I believe I would not be where I am today without The Compassionate Friends. Talking to, writing to and reading about other parents gives me comfort, peace and the strength to look forward into the future without for one moment forgetting Samantha.

As a family we have adjusted to life without Samantha in our own particular ways. I find writing about the experiences helpful and calming, whereas John finds it distressing. He still enjoys his sport, which has always been his release. Nick has a wonderful circle of friends, many being Samantha's too. He has, quite rightly, been able to enjoy his life since his sister died, even though he misses her. Nothing worse than Samantha's death (as bad, but not worse) can happen to John and me, but with it we have been given love, friendship and compassion that we would otherwise never have known.

Jane Morris

ROSIE

Little did I know as I sat with my family on a Welsh beach in August 1985 what lay in store for us. I considered myself very lucky. I had a happy marriage, two lovely daughters – Eleanor, aged eight, and Rosie, six – and a baby son, David, of eight months, a delight to us all, especially to his two adoring sisters.

Looking back on that holiday a sense of foreboding was ever-present. Indeed, six weeks later, our family life was shattered. There was clearly something wrong with Rosie. She was becoming withdrawn and was not content to play with her sister on the beach as she had done in previous years. She had also put on a lot of weight recently, something I could not understand as she had a sparrow's appetite. It was difficult to find anything she enjoyed eating (typical of young children, we were told – so faddy, but they grow out of it). Nevertheless, she was beginning to look as though she had too healthy an appetite and I was baffled.

We returned home from a none-too-successful holiday to await the start of a new term. Towards the end of August Rosie developed a 'viral infection'. She became more lethargic and was prone to sickness and sleeping bouts. She would have a few good days in between and finally returned to school, having missed the first week of term. To my horror, on picking her up one afternoon, I noticed she was squinting. I do not wish to go into detail about the next week or so. Suffice to say, in my heart I was not convinced she was suffering from a mere viral infection, I felt she had a brain tumour and this diagnosis was backed up by information gleaned from the 'brain' section of the *Encyclopaedia Britannica*.

It was a Saturday morning in September when she was

admitted to hospital as an emergency case. My husband, Neil, and I took her in the car. We were questioned; she was examined and later that day was sent for a scan. I shall never forget the moment for as long as I live. We were shown her brain scan and the tumour was pointed out to us by the duty registrar. As my husband and I clung to each other in our grief (I remember there were no chairs, no cups of tea) I felt my heart break and, from that day, I have understood where the expression came from.

Rosie spent seven weeks in hospital in all. She was operated on a week after admission. Her tumour was benign, but large and barely accessible. Neil and I moved into the hospital, leaving my sister to care for the two children at home. Rosie spent the week following her operation 'precariously balanced' – the consultant's phrase, and one that is etched on our memories. She had bad fits twice and did not properly regain consciousness for days – a harrowing time for all her family and friends.

One afternoon, when Rosie was critically ill, Neil at her bedside as usual, I sat in the hospital garden in the autumn sunshine with a friend who said to me that if Rosie should die I should think of the six and a half years of love and happiness she had given me and how worthwhile that had been. I remember, through my tears, saying that the pain of losing her would always outweigh the happiness she had brought us.

Scenes that I had seen only on television became a reality – the child on a ventilator next to Rosie, a road accident victim, and the cassette and 'get well' cards sent from school. We could have opened a toy shop with all the presents she received.

Her 'recovery' began. We became used to the drugs doses and her daily blood test when she screamed in fright every time she saw the nurse. She didn't look like my child any more, with her shaved head, her swollen eyes – one of which did not open again for months owing to bruised nerves – her bloated body and her unhappy expression. The Rosie I knew was a sweet, affectionate little redhead, good-natured and very bright and popular with everyone. This Rosie was a travesty and one I had to get used to.

Back at home, friends and neighbours rallied round to help in every conceivable way – cooking meals, ironing, ferrying people to and from the hospital and looking after Eleanor and David. Rosie was the focus of our lives during that period. Perhaps we did not spend enough time at home, but at the time there was no question in our minds as to where we should be.

On 26 August 1987 Rosie died suddenly at home. She had an epileptic fit and the doctor could not save her. I arrived home an hour later to find a distraught husband and a house full of doctors and weeping friends. I cannot fully describe my feelings – sheer disbelief and agony. Two years of torment had ended like this, with no warning. What had it all been for? I did not watch her die; my husband did and has to live with the memory – the desperate attempts at resuscitation, the feelings of helplessness and the guilt at not being able to save her. To me her actual death was like her second death, one final kick in the teeth. We had already lost our real daughter two years earlier. The real Rosie never reappeared after her operation and we had never successfully readjusted to this initial 'bereavement'.

After the death of a child (or anyone presumably) events assume their own momentum. I do not clearly remember planning her funeral as others did it for us. I remember attending it though; the packed crematorium, the atmosphere of love, unity, friendship and despair. I remember the endless line of mourners afterwards, the disbelieving nurses from Booth Hall Children's Hospital, Judy the minibus lady who escorted Rosie daily to her special school, the care assistants and the staff from the school, not to mention our family and friends who had seen us through it all and stood by so loyally.

Before Rosie's funeral I agonised over whether or not to see her in the chapel of rest. Finally I decided to go. I think I imagined some sort of 'horror scenario' straight out of a Dracula film. I was really afraid. On a suitably macabre note to reinforce my wild imaginings the elderly lady in charge of the chapel of rest greeted us that night by saying that Rosie had actually looked better that day than she had done the previous one! Funny, really, if it hadn't been so sad! I must say, though, that in my experience seeing Rosie after her death helped me to cope with her funeral. In her coffin she was not my child, merely a shell. I have no firm beliefs in an afterlife. I simply do not know what happens when we die. One thing was certain, though – Rosie was no more and I coped better because of this realisation. The funeral was a necessary ritual, that was all.

Three or four days after the funeral Neil, Ellie and I walked to the churchyard down the road and there, in the garden, with the support of the minister, we buried her ashes and planted a rosemary bush in her memory. I think that at times like this there is an internal mechanism which comes into operation and distances you from the actual event in which you are participating. Otherwise, how could such things possibly be bearable?

I think we grieved both quietly and loudly in those early days. My husband cried openly, perhaps more than I did, and why not? Perhaps he proved to all around us that 'real men' are allowed to cry. I do not see it as a sign of weakness. Initially I do not think you are in control of your emotions and have to behave naturally in the circumstances.

Ellie, on being told of her sister's death was hysterical. She sobbed uncontrollably and muttered pathetically, 'She didn't know that I loved her.' It was a cruel, intolerable experience for a ten-year-old without the maturity to handle it. I think from that point on she bottled up her feelings. She didn't want to be treated any differently at school and have attention drawn to her. She did not come to the funeral, which I very much regret. I was the only person who wanted her there but was outvoted by family and friends. What Ellie thinks of this I do not know. It has never been discussed, just like her feelings about losing her sister have never been discussed.

The next few weeks or months passed by somehow. My stomach was always in knots. Friends and neighbours were kind and supportive, but somehow it was easier for them when there was something concrete they could do before Rosie died. We were the ones who needed help now and I believe those who cared about us were in an impossible situation. I was ultra-sensitive (and still am); easily hurt by well-meaning remarks like 'At least you've still got the other two', 'It was a blessing that she died', and so on. Remaining children cannot fill the gap. I know I am lucky to have them, but you do not divide your parental love by the number of children you have.

I gave all Rosie's clothes away soon after she died and we parcelled her toys up and gave them to the hospital and special school. It was perhaps done too hurriedly – I often wish I had kept a 'flower fairy'! A friend helped me to clear her bedroom a couple of weeks after she died. Down came her posters and school photos from the walls. Trinkets and treasured possessions were put away. I have a bedding chest in my bedroom which I think of as 'Rosie's Box'. It is full of mementos: her school work, her drawings, class photos, childish holiday diaries, favourite toys, and also all the get-well cards and letters of sympathy sent after her death. I could not bear to part with them. Although the box lid remains mostly tightly shut, I know I only have to open it to be with her again. Her short life-story is recorded in three photograph albums which Neil is responsible for. He needed to organise our rather chaotic collections of family photos so he did this and these albums are now precious to us.

Looking back, I can now see that Neil and I withdrew from the friendship circles we had been part of, finding it too hard to see Rosie's classmates and other complete families. Better, and less painful, not to bother.

I think our support came from, three or four close friends who have never deserted me. One GP was especially kind to me four months after Rosie's death. He had not been involved at all with our family during Rosie's illness, but was aware of the situation. I was not coping very well and he found time to listen, sensitively and with compassion and encouragement.

We suffered from two classic reactions to bereavement (so the books say): Neil changed his job to make a fresh start and we moved house, not far away, to escape the memories. Both were done hurriedly, without due consideration, and I have my doubts that either was right. The staff at the school where Neil taught were supportive and sympathetic. Neil was absent a lot during the early days of Rosie's illness and used to accompany me to outpatient appointments if friends were unavailable. The school never once stood in his way. They, particularly the Head, emphasised the over-riding importance of 'family' – teaching, after all, is only a job. Somehow, because the staff were so involved, Neil needed to start again, somewhere new. For some reason he wanted his past to be a secret, as Eleanor did, too. He wanted to be on an equal footing with colleagues. He got his wish and was promoted to another school, in a different authority much further away. His anonymity was assured and he seemed to breathe a sigh of relief.

Moving house was even more traumatic. We could not live with the memories of our sick child. We still 'saw' her in every room, 'saw' her drawing at her red table, 'saw' her playing in the garden as the healthy girl she once was. Five months after her death we moved, only half a mile away. I still desperately needed my support network of friends, the total opposite of Neil who needed to close the book on it all publicly! There was, however, also no question of disrupting the children by leaving the area.

On the actual removal day I remember a feeling of deep anxiety – how would Rosie know where we were? Was I completely mad? I don't think so. Recently a friend told me of a widowed friend who is reluctant to move house because her late husband will not know where she is. The very first thing I did on the removal day was to put Rosie's photo on our new mantelpiece. She was the first to arrive in our new home and once she was established there I felt able to cope with the upheaval myself.

We have several photos of Rosie at home. Nothing fancy, just ordinary framed ones, all quite small. I have never felt the need for huge, blown-up prints or oil paintings done from photos. I know many bereaved parents do, and I think it is a personal choice. Rosie loved to do cross-stitch with a kind friend of mine. I have framed a simple sampler, which I shall treasure, and a beautiful poem which she copied. These hang on the wall in the dining room and are there for all to see. I am always pleased if visitors comment on them. On my kitchen wall she smiles out happily, together with her sister, surrounded by sandcastles. I would not like to be without these pictures.

One other source of comfort to me, particularly in the first couple of years, was reading – reading of other people who had lost children and watching any relevant television programmes. I particularly remember a programme about the Alderhey Children's Hospital Centre for Bereaved Parents, which was the first in the country. One father talked movingly about the loss of his nine-year-old daughter; he was speaking my feelings exactly. I love poetry too. In fact, anything that lets me know I am not alone in my grief and anguish.

I read a newspaper article by a widow who derived comfort from writing letters to her deceased husband. I thought this was a good idea and ever since then I have kept a diary as if I am writing to Rosie. I tell her how I feel and what has happened in the family. I do not write in it every day – often weeks or months elapse between entries – but it has helped me. In this diary I also write down quotations which come from all sources – children's poems, Vera Brittain's *Testament of Youth, The Prophet* and, last but not least, The Compassionate Friends' publications.

I discovered The Compassionate Friends a year after Rosie's death, by chance, and greatly valued the newsletters and the friends it has brought me locally. When we meet I feel part of an exclusive club of which I would really rather not be a member! Nevertheless, the atmosphere when we are together is always warm and reassuring and certainly not without humour! We are not at all morbid, just honest and realistic. We spend a great deal of time, as does any group of friends, discussing our families and the trials and tribulations of daily life. Conversation flows naturally, but we know that if we are feeling low or are approaching an anniversary, or one of us has been hurt by an insensitive remark, the others are there to listen and understand. Just meeting another four mothers in my circumstances has helped me enormously.

I have also contacted through TCF a couple whose daughter died at the age of six with exactly the same condition as Rosie. The mother appealed for contacts through the newsletter and I replied. This family lives quite a distance from us, but my husband and I have met up with them midway two or three times and I know we have all benefited from meeting each other and exchanging stories, reactions and feelings. The Compassionate Friends has provided me with the opportunity to form instant friendships in a way unknown to me before. Our bond created by shared experience is so great that things like our interests, backgrounds and so on are irrelevant.

As a family, especially to us as parents the loss of Rosie was devastating. Ellie appears to have blotted out the past and never mentions her sister whom she once loved so dearly. She has a photo of them both together in her room, but I do not know whether she leaves it there for my sake or her own. David has none of the emotional problems the rest of us experience. He was two and a half when she died and does not remember her. He does not mind talking about her and I have found this helpful. I do not want her to be a taboo subject and yet there is an insurmountable barrier with Ellie and a barrier of heartbreak with Neil. We do not comfort each other. We have suffered too deeply through the experience and would only compound one another's unhappiness. We have to look elsewhere for help and support.

Christmas and family holidays are still hard to cope with and it's a relief when they are over. I think, in the early years, you survive them on autopilot. On Rosie's birthday we buy presents for Ellie and David and I always put flowers for Rosie in the church and her name is on view that day in the Book of Remembrance there. The anniversary of her death is, of course, another emotional occasion. I always put a small notice in the 'In Memoriam' column of our local paper. It's as if I'm trying to say we haven't forgotten our dear daughter, even if the rest of you have. She still matters.

Do not think that there is no enjoyment or happiness in my life; there is, but on a more superficial level, I suppose. I can laugh and derive pleasure from occasions as anybody else does, but as Neil once said, 'There is no happiness which is not diminished by the absence of Rosie.' I suppose the difference is that my happiness is never complete. There is always an underlying sadness. To the outside world we must appear to be a 'normal' family. In daily life the majority of people with whom I come into contact now have no idea of my past. I do not feel I am one of them; somehow I am an outcast and cannot be part of their lives.

I do not think I have ever felt angry at losing Rosie. Who should I be angry at, and for what? I cannot blame anyone. The doctors did their best. However, I do find people's well-meaning explanations for why Rosie had to die totally absurd: 'She was too good for this world', 'God wanted her for himself, he only takes the best', and 'You are never given more to bear than you can cope with.' Such sayings do nothing whatsoever to help nor do they provide a meaning or justification for it all. Not for me anyway. I do not feel guilty. If her illness had been diagnosed earlier she would have been operated on earlier. She might still have been alive now, but I do not believe she would have been a healthy, normal child with a bright future ahead of her. Why speculate anyway? Of course I feel guilty in as much as I would have acted differently had I known she would die. She would never have been transferred to a special school – all that emotional and physical upheaval for one term! I would have been more patient; I would have tried harder; I would have coped better . . . if only, if only. There was no way I could have known. We were told she had a normal life expectancy. I never prepared for her death because I was too busy trying to come to terms with her shattered life.

I am probably not the person to convince another bereaved parent that things will get better. Of course the sharp unbearable pain modifies itself until it becomes a constant dull ache. The bad days are fewer, 'normality' takes over. Yes, time heals in a way, although I never thought I would admit this. I know myself now and know which situations I can cope with and which I cannot. I never go to the school harvest festival service. I did once and had to leave because the children sang a hymn that Rosie's class-mates taped for her when she was in hospital. There are still 'trig-gers' and maybe there always will be. You cannot prepare for them all; there will always be the odd, poignant reminder which takes you unawares and plunges you back into sadness and makes the tears well. I cannot listen to music from 'Joseph and His Amazing Technicolor Dreamcoat' because Rosie loved it so much. I could never return to Llanbedrog in North Wales; we had such happy holidays there when the girls were little and to go back would hurt too much. Perhaps I will in time overcome these feelings. I don't know.

I still find it hard to see children who were in Rosie's class at school. I cannot help wondering what Rosie would have been like. As Ellie reaches all the childhood and adolescent milestones – school camp, transfer to secondary school, GCSEs, and now a first driving lesson – I can't help feeling bad about the fact that her sister will never know these joys or trials and will never fol-low in her footsteps.

Of course my perspective on life has changed radically. When I stood in the playground at school, waiting for David, for a long time I felt more comfortable on my own. Any talk of petty, mun-dane problems such as panic over the latest outbreak of chicken-pox used to upset me out of all proportion. Wasting large amounts of emotional energy on seemingly trivial matters irri-tated me, although I am the first to admit that, but for Rosie, I would probably have joined in and been one of them!

I know there are those who think I am 'over it' now, who think you cannot grieve for ever. When I confided in a neighbour about my involvement with The Compassionate Friends some time ago she asked in surprise, 'Oh, does it still bother you then?' Someone else implied that we were lucky not to have a problem in our household now that we did not have to look after Rosie any more. Hurtful remarks such as these will continue, I suppose, along with the silence from friends and relatives who think it is all too sad or happened too long ago to talk about. I love to talk about Rosie. I never want to deny her existence, yet this poses a source of embarrassment to many. I am eternally grateful to the few who bring her naturally into conversations, remember her birthday and mention her readily. It must be hard to do.

I no longer feel I am stuck in my grief although for three years I made little progress and was obsessed by thoughts of Rosie, no matter where I was, at work or at home. It was as if half my mind was permanently preoccupied, leaving the other half to cope with whatever I was supposed to be doing. Books that describe the stages of grief are not at all helpful. I do not believe there is a set pattern for anyone, and I think it is harmful to suggest that if you have not reached a certain stage by a certain time you are suffering from unresolved or pathological grief. The 'expert' authors of these studies have no doubt not shared our experience. Nobody who has not lost a child can know what it is like or has the right to say 'I know how you must feel.' There are questions I cannot answer. Sometimes I do not know what to say when people ask me how many children I have. It depends on who is asking.

I do not think the day has yet come when I can wake up and feel positive. When I wake I feel that I can cope with the day, deal with what lies ahead but the memory of happier times will always be tinged with sadness because those times have gone and will never return. No one could ever express how I feel about things better than this:

When you are sorrowful, look again in your heart and you shall see that in truth you are weeping for that which has been your delight.[6]

In Rosie's primary school, which her brother now attends, hang a picture and a poem in Rosie's memory. The illustrator of her favourite poetry book kindly sent me a print of the picture that illustrated Rosie's favourite poem, 'The Wood of Flowers' by James Stephens. The artist in question has become a friend. I have met her twice and continue to correspond with her. As for 'The Wood of Flowers', that is where I like to imagine my precious daughter, happy and smiling as she used to be when she brought us all so much joy and happiness.

Janet Williamson

PAUL

It is now nearly the same length of time since Paul's death as his life had been, so it is appropriate that I should look back over the last twenty years and write something about how we coped with losing him in April 1975 when he was nearly twenty-one years old. He was our first-born child, born in our second year of marriage, and was soon to be followed by a sister and brother within the next five years.

Paul had been born with a physical handicap; that, and various other long-term problems frequently kept him away from school until he was nearly ten and began to attend a special school.

All the children went to the local secondary modern school and Paul won the prize for the best exam results ever when he left. He later went on to study for an honours degree in a college not far from home. He was unhappy in his first year and decided to leave as his course wasn't relevant to the kind of work he eventually wanted to do, to be a warden on a nature reserve.

After travelling abroad to Ethiopia, which was traumatic, he came home and went on to work as a Community Service Volunteer one-to-one with young mentally handicapped people in a hospital in the North of England. We became quite concerned about him at this time and took him away for a weekend in the Lake District.

Soon after this Paul took his life. We discovered he had made an appointment to see the doctor that same weekend, but had failed to keep it. He left no note, only a photograph on film which we discovered later. Strangely I had felt very disturbed during that weekend, a feeling shared by my sister at the same time, but I had failed to phone Paul.

When I returned home from work and saw my husband's face, I knew what had happened. We had a hurried meal, called to see my parents, sister and our vicar, and rushed off to the hospital where he had worked. The staff at the hospital were very kind and we stayed in a room near Paul's, where we ate our meals, saw the police, coroner, chaplain, funeral directors and registrars. We decided to have the funeral where Paul had chosen to die, and the hospital chapel was full of his fellow volunteers and staff. He was cremated and we held a memorial service in our own church two days later.

I was angry at being prevented from seeing Paul's body by a man at the door who felt I might be too distressed. Afterwards I wished I had scattered the ashes by the badger-set in the woods, where Paul had spent many nights with a friend, but I could not bear the idea of them being sent by post and we couldn't wait for them as we had to get home to our other children.

A number of Paul's old college and school friends turned up for his service, or visited afterwards, and it was more cheerful than I could have imagined with the young members of the family chatting in the kitchen, over the washing-up. A friend thought I ought to have cried at the service, but I would never have regained control if I had let go and would have lost the chance to talk to Paul's friends, some of whom lived some distance away.

Paul had enjoyed photographing birds so we decided to donate a bird bath to the patients at the hospital. Unfortunately, the hospital is now closed, but we do hope our gift is still being used by someone who enjoys birds. As my younger son and I sorted through his belongings, we felt we washed the room with the tears we shed. We gave most of his clothes to charity, although we kept some of them and all of his books.

A week after we first heard the news we went back to work as I had examination marks to hand in and my own children were doing 'O' and 'A' Levels. Friends called to accompany them and I had a friend who was recently bereaved herself, who travelled with me, and we found it a great solace to talk. In fact we both felt we would have found it very difficult by ourselves. Another friend encouraged me to go to church with her, although I usually cried throughout the service, but nobody seemed to mind.

Going home was difficult after trying to control myself all day, so I used to visit my parents or other people, before picking up my husband and going home with him. I was also contacted by one or two Compassionate Friends, but it was three years before I visited a family myself who had lost a child through suicide. I felt tremendous relief at finding someone else with the same challenge. This mother and father had also lost a baby and a small child and survived. If I had no one from The Compassionate Friends to visit I found acquaintances who, although not personally distressed by our loss, were willing to listen or wanted to talk themselves.

I remember hearing a woman on television, whose husband had been killed, saying that she had no time to grieve at the moment, and I knew what she meant, as all the time is taken up just keeping going and caring for the family. I longed for a 'wailing wall' where I could go and scream to high heaven – a silent sob is not enough.

Through The Compassionate Friends some of us took part in a writing circle, adding a letter to the packet as it came round and removing the previous one. The founder member handed it on to me for two or three years and I finally met her unexpectedly at a retreat house a long way from home. Someone who had lost a child herself told me to keep doing the things I planned, even though it might seem difficult or as if I was being unfeeling; I think it proved good advice. I remember taking an embroidery to an exhibition, which means nothing to me now, but at the time provided a contact with an encouraging organiser and led on to other activities involving my daughter too.

At first I forced myself to speak to neighbours, as they found it difficult to approach us. I felt as though I was in a hovercraft, gliding over a very rough sea, but lifted above it by the prayers of many people who had seen the report in the papers. Later the grief seemed a castle wall, unassailable, with everyone else on the other side. People do not need to talk; just touching your arm or catching your eye is enough. It makes such a difference as you can feel so shut out by grief.

On the first anniversary of Paul's death my husband arranged a surprise visit to Paris. I was a bit unnerved as I had never been there before, but later I realised that Paul would have approved as he enjoyed travel himself. I think one of the reasons he chose not to concern us about his health was because he wanted us to live our own lives adventurously and perhaps felt his illness would have hindered us.

My husband became ill again with osteo-arthritis, as well as his former rheumatoid arthritis, and has had two knee replacements and a pacemaker fitted, as well as other problems; I'm never really sure how much all this was brought on by Paul's death.

I feel I was fortunate to have all Paul's childhood while one of my neighbours never had the chance to know her child as he was so young when he died. However, she now has five other sons, while those of us who are much older cannot have more; not that I think other children can ever replace the child you have lost.

In our family we have all coped with our grief differently. My son left school and moved to college in a nearby town where he moved into a flat with some student friends a few years later. He was active in the local youth theatre and other activities. He moved on to a larger regional college and was president of the union there, so I felt he coped well despite the loss of his brother whom he idolised. He also had a friend in my daughter's boyfriend who spent a lot of time with us.

My husband found that no one in his office spoke to him about his grief – perhaps men find this difficult – although he had spent time listening to their problems and found it very hard that he couldn't talk to them when he needed to.

My daughter, who was eighteen, was distressed by the newspaper report on Paul, but to the reporter it was just a piece about a local tragedy. She phoned the editor to complain that it was not a true picture of her brother. Soon afterwards, her boyfriend, who is an only child, lost his mother, aged forty, and they talked together and helped one another in that way. He and his father came to us at Christmas and my daughter was often at their house, helping them and so helping herself, I imagine.

Paul and I had shared the same sense of humour and enjoyed doing the same things, so I felt very close to him. I had felt depressed too at his age, but had always told him how glad I was now to enjoy so much in life and have my family.

Paul told me he would never marry or have children and asked me why I had brought him into a world full of sorrow. Later, he asked me if I would mind if he went far away and, although I guessed what he was saying, I told him I thought he might work abroad one day, but I would miss him, of course. In a way I know I was giving him permission and have always felt ridden with guilt, but I feel he wanted us to be happy and perhaps felt he was causing us distress by creating tension in the house. I knew I must encourage my other children to travel and leave home as they grew older, but my daughter found college in London depressing and one of her tutors, whose sister had taken her own life, advised me to get her moved nearer home. This time I intervened and saw the principal and she was moved home again to travel daily to a college nearby where she did very well, later gaining a degree.

Almost immediately, following the horror and distress, I knew the only way to mitigate them was to use the experience positively in some way, not only for myself, but also for Paul. Perhaps we only need to be ready, because six months afterwards, someone asked me to help a group of homeless people in a nearby town. A house was being rented from the council, but the only helpers were unpaid volunteers, so much help was needed practically, but also in listening and supporting. Many people could have been in their position, with problems such as divorce or unemployment putting the family into a crisis situation.

Both our surviving children now have happy families and live
away from us, but make regular visits, as does my mother, who is
now widowed. I think bereavement is like losing a limb, a part of
oneself that can never be replaced, but that we can be helped to
accept and come to terms with it as we progress through life. I
have been helped by people and had opportunities to help people,
often being asked to visit the bereaved, and I feel I can now listen
with greater understanding. I attended a bereavement counselling
course, which my school sent me on, to help children cope with
loss. I also work on other courses for victim support and media-
tion dealing with neighbourhood problems. Although we feel at
first that we have lost everything, it has some value in that sometimes it can be used as an experience to give understanding to
others in their times of sorrow. Two family friends had husbands
who became very ill a year or so after we lost Paul, one with MS
and the other with Alzheimer's disease. Both were in their mid-
fifties. They were both pleased to have a visit and I was perhaps
able to enliven their day a little with stories from school – they
had been teachers – and it helped me to cope better having
laughed at our problems.

I was pushed into being chairman of the Ideal Homeless
Group after a couple of years and continued for ten years, finally
leaving after seventeen interesting years. My younger son was
also on the management committee for a time and is now managing a number of houses elsewhere in the country, having originally trained for a different career. I hope I gave something as I
myself was given so much and enjoyed being involved with so
many lives at a time when my own children were leaving home.
Strangely, one young female worker from Denmark became a
friend at a time when my daughter was living in Copenhagen.

Several young people came into our lives at this time, five of
them having lost a mother. Some asked to be like another son and
I felt God had meant us to meet and help each other at this point
in time. They send us pictures of their families now and I feel
grateful also to Paul's friends who still write to us each year and

send a card at Christmas. I can give them an annual report of local news!

About a fortnight after the funeral it was Paul's twenty-first birthday. Strangely I had insisted we celebrate his eighteenth birthday 'in case he wasn't around at twenty-one', thinking it was likely he would be away at that age. I had not mentioned it to anyone, but felt I could not sit in the canteen eating lunch with the school on such a day, so I just walked away in the middle of the meal to hide. A young teacher, who had just lost her father, rushed after me to talk and persuaded me to return. The other teacher on the table had recently lost an adopted baby so we all had a loss, but it was still difficult to talk under the circumstances.

I was able to use some of my experiences while visiting the bereaved for the church, as church warden, for a few years. Retiring was also a difficult time as in some way you feel with so much more time all the suppressed feelings will come back. However, I had the opportunity to do a diploma course in theology at university. This occupied my spare hours in the first three years, by which time I was used to occupying myself and wondered how I had ever had time to work.

I still cry for Paul, especially if I wake up in the early morning, but I must be thankful for the other people who have come into our lives – Paul's best friend, a medical student, was posted nearby and had the key to our home so that he could visit any time when he was in a hospital nearby for several years.

We kept some personal things of Paul's and some of his little treasures; we still use some items of his clothing, like his duffle coat for gardening or walking and several shelves of books. His brother and sister obviously used some of the things he had owned which they found useful to them.

We have a photograph of Paul in our bedroom and there are many photos of him in albums. I gave my son and daughter a special album of family pictures, particularly of them, when they left home to have a family of their own.

The grandchildren refer to Paul naturally and I have made
them some little books over the years about things such as the
family adventures and pets. I want them to know about all the
happy times we had together and they like looking through the
albums with me occasionally. However, we had not looked at the
slides Paul had made of his travels since he had shown them to us
a few months before he died. His brother mentioned them and
finally organised us into watching them again, which was
painful, but also important accepting again that he remains for
ever young in our memory, while our other children are nearing
middle age.

The eldest grandchild inherited Paul's handicap so that at all
the other family births there has been some anxiety for all of us.
Paul was very fond of children and they would run to meet him
when he came along the road, and sing songs. He also looked
after them in the evenings when neighbours wanted to go out, as
did his brother and sister later, and my mother-in-law who lived
with us – we could always supply a babysitter!

I realise I have so much to be grateful for and the memory of a
very dear and loving son, who I feel is not so far away. I recently
found the following lines from a prayer, which I think are important in our healing:

> *God, please help me to know that every moment, no matter
> what the situation or circumstances, I have a choice between
> Heaven and Hell; between the path of gratitude, acceptance,
> trust, faith, hope, love and the path of resentment, denial,
> judgement, doubt, fear and control.*[7]

Anne Hammond

PETER

It was 26 November 1989, a Sunday lunchtime, when my big strong husband of thirty-nine dropped dead from a heart attack.

Life had never been easy. We both had difficult childhoods and my mother's illness put a big strain on our marriage, but we loved each other and were happy most of the time. We were married for nine years before our beautiful son, Peter, was born. When I came out of hospital Pat took the baby along the corridor and left me struggling with the bags! He had what he had always wanted, his baby son.

He was a wonderful father. He would get up in the night, change nappies, do everything possible. We really shared Peter and were blissfully happy. When Peter was a few months old we moved from the little house we had on the main road because we did not think it would be safe when Peter was older. We bought a house right on top of a park. It was our park. After Pat died I found walking in the park almost unbearable, but I had to do it to take Peter, who was eight years old, to school.

Peter was my strength when his father died. He had seen everything. He saw his father drop dead and saw me screaming as I tried to revive him. It was so public as it happened out in the street. We needed counselling and I had a counsellor called Nick Tyndall who helped to get Peter to talk about his father. After six months, we were eventually coping.

When Pat died I thought nothing could ever hurt as much as losing the man I loved. I totally relied on him for everything. How could anything be more painful than that?

Ten months after Pat's death it was my little girl, Sarah's third birthday. I watched Peter and Sarah laughing in the sunshine and

I can remember thinking Peter *can* be happy without his father. Peter and his father had been so close I didn't think it was possible, but here he was, so happy. He was always telling me how he would help me look after his little sister. Walking through the park on the way to school on 13 September 1990, in the autumn sunshine, he put Sarah over his shoulder, showing how pleased he was that he was now strong enough to do this.

When I collected Peter from school we went on the bus instead of going through the park as we usually did, as we had to return a video. We were talking on the bus about when Peter was older and coming home on his own. He said he would cross at the lights, but I told him that he would have to cross at the zebra crossing. We came out of the video shop and were talking about Peter crossing the road on his own again and he said he would cross at the lights by the park, so I told him again that it would be dangerous and the proper place to cross was on the crossing. I told him to wait until all the traffic stopped and to show me how he would cross the road properly.

I watched my lovely son walk proudly to the kerb and wait until the traffic stopped for him. The car in the nearside lane stopped and when Peter stepped off the kerb I could see one car length in the outside lane was clear. This was a double crossing and the traffic in the second half had already stopped for Peter. I watched him walk out on to the crossing; he even checked when he was halfway across and then continued to walk. He was three-quarters of the way across, almost to the central reservation, when I glanced down at my three-year-old daughter as we were about to follow him across together. As I looked down there was a sound, like an explosion. When I looked up my little son's body was lying crumpled forty yards up the road. A van had stopped just past his body. The driver didn't even know he had hit Peter. He didn't even brake until he was about ten yards past the crossing. If we had all crossed, all three of us would have been killed. From my point of view, and Sarah's, this would have been much better.

Peter was taken to the local hospital where my husband had been taken just ten months earlier. He died twenty-one hours later. I shall always feel that a large part of me also died then. My son had represented everything to me, a link with my husband whom I still love very much.

My daughter saw it all and used to blame me for what happened to her brother. My little Sarah has lost so much – a lovely father and a lovely brother – that I owe it to both of them to try to keep her happy, but she gets very lonely and sometimes I find it very difficult to cope.

It took twelve months for the case to come to court. The driver was found guilty of reckless driving and was banned for four years. I will never forgive him for his arrogant behaviour in the court and the fact that he has never even said sorry for killing my lovely son.

At Peter's school they put a sundial in the garden with the words 'To celebrate the life of Peter O'Brien'. I go there every few months to plant flowers or bulbs, but I still find it very difficult. I do feel lucky to have had my son, even if it was only for a little while.

It is now coming up to four years since Peter was killed. In the early days I think the pain of losing a loved one is physical as well as mental. For me the pain across my chest was sometimes unbearable.

As my son was killed in a road accident I became involved with a new group called RoadPeace. They try to help people in my situation. I did television interviews in my home and at the studio and spoke to newspapers and magazines, all to get some coverage for RoadPeace. Sometimes it would set me back for weeks to relive the accident, but I had to keep on doing it because I felt it was something I could still do for Peter so that people would not forget him.

My son was a gentle person, like his father, and very placid. Sometimes I feel guilty for feeling so angry at the world for his death. I felt so guilty about him crossing the road on the zebra crossing. I believed for about three months that it was all my fault and it was because I was a useless mother that I had allowed my son to be killed. But with counselling I realised that in this life you do not have complete control over every other person's actions.

Other people's comments would make me so angry. The court case was put off to allow the person that killed Peter to take his exams at university and the police inspector said, 'But don't forget he's studied hard for them.' He did not stop to think that was something my little boy was never going to be able to do!

If friends did not speak about the death of my child I would just start talking about him. After they realised that I could speak about him, they gradually became braver and started to mention him. I would keep looking through the pictures over and over again, remembering Peter smiling and enjoying himself. I have a lot of photographs around. I used to worry that my husband and my son having died would be too much for other people to cope with. They might think of my home as morbid, but my friends assure me that it's part of my life and to have all the photos out is not unnatural. So, I find a lot of comfort from them now, but in the early days the pain was so great that I could only stand to have one out at a time.

When my son died all his toys and clothes were given to a children's home by his cub scout group, but every now and then one of his cars or soldiers turns up, mixed in with my daughter's toys. I don't get the searing pain I used to. I just remember how happy he was playing with them.

My little girl would come and cuddle me in the early days – certainly during the first two years. When I cried a lot of the time we would both cry together, but I had professional advice on how to help Sarah because of her losing her father and then, ten months later, actually seeing her brother killed in such a violent way. I talked to Sarah, this little three-year-old girl, about her brother all the time. She would worry that he did not have any toys in heaven. She would ask questions all the time as she grew.

It was very wearing, but I was told this was best for her. Today she is nearly seven and is a happy, confident little girl, and she has happy memories of her lovely brother and her father.

I would always talk to children about anyone they have lost, but only when they want to do it. If they don't want to talk about it on one particular occasion, try again another day. I know with my daughter she had good days and bad days, like me. I found talking to other bereaved parents, and writing, extremely helpful. I didn't feel I was the only one; someone else really knew how I felt.

I am a much stronger person now than I was before. I get more into life for myself and my daughter than I did before. I really try to concentrate on what I had and what Peter had in his short life. He was a very loved, happy child. As we all know too well, there are children all over this world who don't have this luxury. There used to be places, like his school, that I couldn't cope with, but it is true that the more you do things the easier they get. Not that it is really easy, just more bearable.

After my son's death we moved about two miles away. I still go to the same school for my daughter and see all the same people, but I can cope better now. I think moving helped us a lot. On birthdays and anniversaries I try to remember Pat and Peter in happy ways. One year I took my little girl to a big theme park which I used to go to with Peter. It was painful, but happy as well. Another year I went and sat for ages in the park, by the flowers where Peter learned to walk. I think people should do whatever is right for them to remember their loved ones, as I believe they are with you all the time and always will be.

Rosalie O'Brien

DAVID

The summer of 1983 was very hot. David, our elder son, was twenty and home from Liverpool University helping my husband John and me in our small business. Although both physicists, we were in fact running a small industrial pottery. Paul at eighteen was just completing his first year in a job with British Rail. Deborah, our youngest, was fifteen and just thinking about next year's 'O' Level exams.

During that summer I spent a lot of time with David, both at home and at work. I remember thinking, 'Whatever happens I have had this time', and I treasured it.

Living in the country meant both boys had motorbikes for transport, so I knew all about sitting up in the small hours fearing the worst. When it happened it was 8.15 on the one wet morning of that very sunny August. David had come home from a holiday the night before and stayed in Cambridge. As I went to work I remember thinking, 'I believe at last I have got used to them riding motorbikes.' At that moment he was probably lying unconscious beside the road. An outpatient at the local psychiatric hospital had stepped out from behind a bus straight under his wheels. David wasn't speeding but neither of them had a chance. The patient's illness caused her to be disorientated; perhaps the rain distracted her – we will never know. She was killed outright; David was rushed to hospital.

Deborah opened the door to the policeman and she rang us at work. For months I had trouble answering the phone early in the morning, especially on a Wednesday, the day the accident happened. We rushed to the hospital where the police explained to us what had happened. The policeman seemed very unsympathetic, obviously blaming David because he was on a motorbike. The policewoman on the other hand was a very sympathetic person; she visited us in our home afterwards and was the only professional who really offered any support. At the hospital we met the admissions doctor, who was accompanied by a nurse. He explained that David was in intensive care with massive head injuries and that although he would like to give us hope, he couldn't. I give him great credit for telling us the truth; it helped me to come to terms with the inevitable.

We seemed to wait for ages (about five hours) in an alcove in the corridor outside the neurological intensive care annexe. John remembered that David had wanted to be an organ donor. The duty doctor produced a form for our peace of mind but 'didn't think it would come to that'. Eventually we were allowed to see David – they had spent all that time 'stabilising' him. He was lying attached to a ventilator, covered by a metal sheet, and appeared to be breathing normally. But it didn't really look like David. We were told he was too deeply unconscious for us to do any good by talking to him.

It was really no surprise – although we hoped against hope – when we were called to the consultant's room next morning. He explained that David was brain-dead, although his heart was being kept beating by the ventilator. If for us true death was heart death they would keep David on the ventilator till his heart stopped, which usually took a few days. When he was satisfied we accepted brain death – and only then – did he accept our offer of organ donation. Oddly enough, his most helpful statement was that even if we hoped for a miracle and David survived he would never see or hear again as his eyes and ears had been destroyed.

We both chose not to go back to the intensive care unit. To us David had already gone; only a shell was left. Later we decided to see David in the chapel of rest, but once the funeral director had seen David he advised us against it. I have been made to feel unnatural about this decision not to look at the body, but I believe it was right for me. I also know of people who have been advised against viewing the body and afterwards bitterly regretted it. It has to be a matter of personal choice.

So we went home to break the news. Although we had all known how serious the accident was, we had all hoped against hope that a miracle would happen. I had even planned converting our extension to nurse David. We rang the local doctor as we were concerned for John's invalid parents who lived across the road. He advised us to 'break the news gradually'. How do you do that? He said he would not prescribe anything for them as they – indeed, all of us – would be better off coming to terms on our own. We accept that he was right. John tried a triple brandy – he doesn't normally drink – but it did nothing so he didn't bother with alcohol again.

Paul was told about David's death by the nurses as he visited the hospital on his way home from work. Deborah just couldn't believe it at first. We had advised her against visiting David because we thought his appearance might be too much for her to cope with and later felt she would be better remembering him as he was. I still don't know if we were right or wrong. We had to tell his girlfriend Saskia over the phone and she went to say her goodbyes. The local rector rang up to see how David was and when we told him he was dead he didn't know what to say!

On Friday the theatre nurse rang to say the ventilator had been shut off. For John this was the final event – for me David had been dead since Wednesday. Until we received the death certificate several months later we didn't know on which day he legally died. In fact it is normal practice to sign the certificate after the second of two sets of brain-death tests.

The following Monday (a bank holiday – the day we'd planned a rare family outing) John went to collect David's belongings from the hospital and asked if David had been able to be a donor. The junior administrator on duty was eventually able to discover that David had donated heart, kidneys, pancreas and liver (his eyes were damaged and this was before the days of lung transplants). I will never forget the euphoria I felt when

John told me this news. The elation didn't last long but the fact that David was able to help these people has been of great support over the years. David had been talking of his wishes only a few days before he died (we later found about ten donor cards in his belongings). Although the accident had really been her fault, I still felt guilt that the patient would not have died if David had not been there at that moment, so it was important to me that he had saved other lives.

Our neighbours and friends were comforting. One just came to the door, gripped our hands and went away; he felt too deeply to speak, but that was enough. All the letters, cards and visits were of great help, in particular a letter from the daughter of the dead patient saying simply, 'I'm so sorry.' We read and reread these letters, learning about the existence of university friends we had never heard of. Although it made us cry, at the same time we were proud to know how well he was thought of and what joy he had brought to others by just being his own fun-loving self.

In the days leading up to the funeral we lived in an unreal world almost as if we were watching ourselves grieve. The paradox was that I had longed for a quiet time in my very busy life and now I had it! Saskia spent much of her time with us and we clung to our two children and her. Both John and Saskia found comfort in lying on David's bed to feel his nearness. In these early days we spent hours listening to his music. We moved his hi-fi downstairs as I couldn't bear to listen to the sounds of his music coming from upstairs, thinking of all the times I had complained about the volume. Ever since then I think we have gained comfort from and been more appreciative of 'his kind' of music. In fact he liked most music, but I will never hear Queen's 'Bohemian Rhapsody' without 'remembering'. His current favourite was 'Jupiter' from the *The Planets* suite, and we thought of having this at the funeral. However, in the end we decided to have a very traditional funeral with an old friend, who used to take the boys sailing, playing the organ. The whole family was involved in planning the funeral. It was very important that David had a good 'send off' and to do everything he would have wanted. It was Saskia who knew he wanted to be cremated. The rector allowed us to bury him in the churchyard with a little plaque and we gained some comfort from the beautiful coloured trees he would be 'looking at'. Later on we placed a seat there in his memory. We decided on donations to Addenbrookes, the local hospital, for microsurgery (David had had an operation on his hand a few years previously). We were grateful for the help of friends who prepared food for the funeral.

It was a great help to us that David's friends from university came down for the funeral. Amazingly we could laugh at the tales of David's exploits. The night before the funeral we went to see the coffin in the church in a side chapel. I remember taking a red rose from the garden as David loved red. Not having viewed the body, this was my moment of truth – David was in there! I never knew what happened to the rose, but I think I truly accepted the death at that moment!

The morning of the funeral was the coldest for months so I dressed in a suit and didn't even notice that by lunchtime it was sweltering. The short journey to the church seemed a farce and I felt as if David were laughing with me at all the ceremony and fuss. During the service I received a hidden strength – perhaps from all the generations who had prayed in that old church and my own religious upbringing – and somehow I got through it. It was a great comfort to see so many people from the village at the funeral, his old school and scout troop as well as his (and our own) friends. We had only close family flowers (red and white – David's colours); at the crematorium David's flowers were beside those of the lady who died with him! Later we had a very small family service when we buried the casket in the church-yard. John got satisfaction in clearing the site and digging the grave himself. This was the last duty he could perform for David.

In the next weeks we found we often had to be the comforters and tell friends and acquaintances how to help us. Most assumed we would want to be alone with our grief, thinking that talking

would 'remind us'; as if we ever forgot! In those days we wanted
to talk and talk. I used to have an hour or so of my own 'space'
between Paul going to work and the other two coming down, and
I often spent this time talking, in effect, to myself – sometimes to
my friends who lived at a distance and sometimes to David himself. I wrote long letters as well. John kept a diary of his feelings
and experiences. Often in those early days we wanted the company of those who had known him to share all the memories,
especially the funny things. Saskia was with us much of the time
and we all clung together in mutual grief. Her parents were very
new friends, but were also of support at the time. The girls at
work kept the business going for John and me.

The whole house seemed to have an atmosphere of gloom.
When David first died John wanted to close the curtains, but I
knew David loved the sunlight and hated being shut in. To begin
with we couldn't watch TV, but after a few days found it helpful
as a background, yet somehow most programmes seemed to be
about some tragedy or other. Again in the first few weeks I could-
n't read, but gradually reading became a way of 'losing myself'.
I really felt I was making progress when I began to knit again.
We still found ourselves viewing ourselves as if we were other
people and watching how we coped.

At times I felt as if I had to live for David now – enjoy the sun,
sky and clouds, eat food and spend money! Just before he died
David had commented on the pleasures of 'spending money and
having nice things', and I got an odd pleasure out of buying
things (we had been careful with money for so long and tried to
make David the same). At other times I felt so guilty I could do
these things and he couldn't. Often we felt he was in the back
seat of the car with us or 'just behind' our shoulder. This feeling
faded after a time and we are both convinced we 'left him
behind' on a visit to Liverpool. We seemed to live on a different
time-scale from everyone else. I remember suddenly being aware
of dark nights and autumn colours, although part of me was still
in that blazing hot August.

At this time we found we were incessantly thinking from the moment we opened our eyes – when immediately the leaden weight of memory dropped on us – till we fell asleep about eighteen hours later out of sheer exhaustion. Physical exercise helped – I remembering 'attacking' the heavy frosting in the freezer with a carving knife. Saskia's speciality was physical education, and she would play games till she all but dropped. Just before David died we had bought a BBC computer, and in fact the last night David was at home he and John were up till one o'clock in the morning playing computer games. For the first time in nine months or so we spent hours playing games. We also joined Prestel, which is in effect an electronic newspaper accessed by the telephone line, so we could read 'bulletin boards' and enter competitions. All our senses were fully occupied and this was a great help to us.

John cleared up David's room quite soon. Although he had been home from university almost a month, most of his belongings were either still packed or strewn around the room. We are glad we kept some of the more personal things. We still have treasured mementos. John still keeps up David's habit of saving pennies in a sweet jar. At the same time we got a strange comfort from Paul wearing some of his clothes. We buried him in the red leather jacket he was so proud of. Presents from David and his woodwork plant-holder and cabinet are important. His hi-fi (with additions) is still in the living room with the kit speakers he made while recovering from microsurgery on his hand. We have now made tape recordings of his records and given Paul the originals.

It was a sadness to us how few photographs we had of David in his older years. Luckily Saskia had lots of snaps, including some from his last holiday, developed after he died. To begin with we found it good to look at these, but then for a while it was very difficult. With the passage of time we are so glad we have them to remind us of happy times. We have never had lots of family photos on show and have not altered this habit, but we know many get great comfort from such displays.

After a few weeks it was over for everyone else so it was expected to be over for us. Even a close friend after three weeks asked, 'Everything OK now?' No, it will never be OK, and in fact you feel still worse once the numbness has worn off, but you can't say so. Even worse was an acquaintance who felt it was all right as we had other children. The most unhelpful comment, from more than one person was, 'I bet you wish you had never let him have a motorbike.' People would worry about small things which to us no longer seemed important.

We felt angry with David for 'doing this' to us and with God for having dealt us this blow. Why did it have to be him, who everyone loved and who would never hurt anything? There were dark thoughts: 'Why couldn't it have been me . . .?' We went through so many 'If onlys . . .', but we know that he had to live his own life. Only a few days before he died he had said, 'I'll take reasonable precautions, but if anything should happen at least I've enjoyed life.'

October came and David's friends went back to Liverpool without him.

We kept thinking 'Things will be better after the inquest', for which we waited three months. The need to know every possible detail was very strong. In fact we found it very unsettling as it was held in the mental hospital – a very gloomy and foreboding building outside which the accident took place. There was really only one witness (on a road full of cars carrying commuters to work) although we later found several local people who had been at or near the scene. I still carry the picture in my mind of David's last conscious moments as described by this witness. It made me feel very close to David. Even so there will always be questions that could only be answered by David himself. Yet after a time the actual events ceased to be of any importance.

I feel lucky I had John and my family to share my grief with. We were sometimes out of phase and this could cause stress and upsets, but these were usually short-lived. With John I knew I had one person who truly understood how I felt. Yet some of our reactions were quite different. I am a person who normally cries at the slightest thing, yet during that time John cried much more than me. I found most comfort in the love of my family and looking after them, whereas John admits that at that time his love for the rest of us was swamped by his grief for David. I felt a great comfort in the familiar routine of work. My work at the pottery involved organising day-to-day production and unloading and reloading kilns. Most of the time I had company. By a quirk of fate two of David's schoolfriends came to work for us at the time, and I could reminisce and almost forget he wasn't back at Liverpool. Much of John's work involved printing transfers on his own on the top floor with the hoist David had helped him install beside him. The pottery was full of fresh equipment he had helped with during that month and often John could not print for tears and resented having to go to work.

Initially John directed his energies by campaigning to get the bus diverted through the mental hospital grounds to try and stop our tragedy happening to anyone else. We were told this was impossible. Five years – and two deaths – later the buses were diverted and we felt we had played at least some small part.

Paul showed very little. He admitted to finding it difficult riding home after visiting David that last day. He admitted to crying in the loo and falling asleep in the bus shelter outside the pub the night of the funeral. He tried very hard to please us. He cut his long hair off and bought 'smart' clothes for the funeral. I feel guilty that we asked it of him, but I hope it was of comfort to him pleasing us. The weekend after the funeral he and John put the roof on the house extension that they had all been building. We had sold the bike David had the accident on and used the money to buy a bike for the local training group, but Paul repaired and rode David's second bike with pride and passed his test two weeks later. He carried on with his job and part-time studies for some time, but said he often wondered if it was worth it – life was too short!

Deborah and I have always been close. She says that she felt that as well as losing her brother she had lost her mother, father and family life as they had been before. Also she felt cheated of the expected sister-in-law and nieces and nephews. I have a similar feeling of extended bereavement in that I also lost my chance of being a grandparent to the children David might have had. Deborah did not openly grieve. As well as starting her 'O' Level year she filled every moment of her time by taking part in a school play and finding a new boyfriend. Nevertheless, at a party that Christmas she became so upset that we had to collect her. David had been a music-loving party-goer and the atmosphere had been too much.

The thing that most upset and angered both children after David's death was an article in the local paper after the inquest which implied David was at fault, just because he was on a motorbike.

It was hard for John's parents who two years earlier had moved close to us for support. John's father had lost his short-term memory and for some time would wake up knowing something awful had happened and Mum had to tell him all over again. Soon the horror penetrated and he stopped asking, but it was tacitly agreed we didn't talk of David to John's father so his mother had to carry much of her grief on her own.

We found the run-up to the first Christmas hard, the lights, the music, the whole atmosphere. Oddly, this would have been our first Christmas without David as he had planned a skiing holiday. But after all our fears that first Christmas and Boxing Day were very peaceful and restful. We still kept the normal 'festivities' but did not sit at the table so we were not so aware of the empty chair. Rather than watch TV all the time we played a new adventure computer game that everyone could join in. The week after Christmas was not so good; we had arranged several family visits, but were very conscious that we were trying too hard to do different things.

In January, John's aunt in Wales, who had looked after him for five years when he was an evacuee during the war, died. All I could think of at her funeral was David. This was to be followed in the next two years by the death first of John's other Welsh aunt and then his father. We found it difficult to mourn as we normally would – our emotions were exhausted.

We tried visiting a medium who came up with some interesting statements. We felt she was genuine, but were left undecided. She told us that a lady in our village was the spiritualist church secretary, and we attended a few services and went to a few 'circles' in her house. The trouble was that John and I were so tired that often the relaxed atmosphere sent us to sleep! I know that a lot of people get comfort from 'contact' with their loved ones, but while I believe there is something 'beyond', I am still unsure of my feelings. I know that John's mother often 'sees' David – one Christmas, while listening to 'Bohemian Rhapsody', she saw him proudly pointing at his speakers; she had no idea of the associations. Personally I have had no direct experience.

Within three months of David dying we discovered The Compassionate Friends. Although initially we had contacted them with the idea of helping others we discovered what a help it was to us to talk to people who had been through a similar experience. We were already feeling isolated – as if it had happened only to us – and here was somewhere you didn't have to pretend as you did to the rest of the world. The leaflets, books and newsletters were also helpful. We made several friends through TCF and continued our association over the years in the hope that we in our turn could help by showing that eventually you do reach a new normality, which might be as good and rewarding, but different.

Being a donor family was a great source of support, but also increased the feeling of being on our own. We felt we would like to set up a group similar to The Compassionate Friends for donor families. Thus, in February 1984, the British Organ Donor Society (BODY) was formed. We soon realised that such a group could be of help to recipients of organs as well, so our committee had donor, recipient, professional and uninvolved members. We

were really unprepared for all the interest this group aroused. By
March we were struggling to answer a postbag of over five hundred letters as a result of articles in the *British Medical Journal*,
the *Guardian* and *The Sunday Times* – all on a portable type-
writer. We soon mastered the 'delights' of simple word-process-
ing and compiled some leaflets. This was accompanied by radio
and TV appearances. I can remember the thrill of being on the
same programme as Roger Daltry – David's hero from the pop
group The Who.

To begin with all this was a help. We felt we were doing something for David. We realise now that this drive is common to
bereaved people but does fade into apathy after a time – few professionals expected our group to last. Normal advice is to wait
two years before starting anything new, but by then the drive has
gone! We did find that we were far too vulnerable to thoughtless
acts and comments. By the summer we realised we needed to
reduce our activity to give ourselves same 'space'. By devoting
so much time to the society we had inadvertently made it seem to
our family that we cared more for David dead than them living.
Nevertheless, it was in those first two months of BODY that for
the first time I began to wake up sometimes with some sort of
pleasant anticipation of the day's events instead of having that
awful sinking feeling.

On David's twenty-first birthday a letter arrived saying that he
(and Paul and Deborah) had each been left £1000 in John's aunt's
will. We kept thinking how thrilled he would have been. I had
not really anticipated this as a bad day so it was probably worse
than other anniversaries, ending up in a row about something
completely unimportant.

On the anniversary of David's death we went to the
Liverpool Garden Festival. A few weeks earlier, in one of our
Prestel competitions, we had won two tickets to the festival and
the next day we saw an advert for a bus trip there, on the
anniversary of the day David died. This seemed as if it was
meant – David had always loved Liverpool. Even now we find

that time of the year unsettling, but that first anniversary has very pleasant memories.

It is now nearly eleven years since David died and we have achieved our new normality. We still think of David with pride and love. We can still feel that lump in the throat at some small unexpected happening and when we talk to or hear of other bereaved families. But we can remember happy times without the same sadness and now find our new life very rewarding.

After several years 'conforming', Paul's love of the more bohemian life took over and he now does contract work to allow him time to travel and work on the fringe of the pop music 'scene'. After two motorbike accidents (one in Denmark) he has finally given up motorcycling. At the moment he is staying in Indonesia and has a girlfriend out there.

Deborah has said she felt she never grieved properly and for several years had difficulty settling down. She now has an MSc, a responsible job, a fiancé and a mortgage, but David's death has left a lasting impression on her life.

Saskia moved back home with her family, went to college and started her career. Recently we were very pleased to be invited to her wedding. We have never managed to set up local groups of BODY as TCF has done, so still handle most of the contacts on the phone. We also try to help recipients and waiting recipients, often by putting them in contact with an appropriate person. Over the years we have become established as a source of information for involved families, the public, the media and professionals, particularly nurses. There is a tree adoption scheme for involved families and an annual convention attended by members and nurses. Recently we have been funded to put on a series of 'road-shows' for nurses about transplantation.

BODY was started to channel our energies and as a memorial to David. We obtained great satisfaction although it was hard work. As the years have gone by, the society has taken more of our time, so we now operate the pottery as a cottage industry and let the building. Our work takes us round the country attending conferences and talking to nurses. We have met well-known people we would never have expected to meet, but by far the most important comfort in our grief has been trying to help others. When the local TCF group disbanded for lack of contacts we became Cambridgeshire county contacts and run the Cambridge group. An unexpected spin-off of trying to help other people is that you help yourself on the way.

Last year at The Compassionate Friends service we all received red roses 'in remembrance'. Two days later, on the hottest day of the summer, John and I toiled up Snowdon, by what to us was a difficult route, to leave our red rose at the summit. We had reached the top of our long uphill struggle since David's death, and this was a reminder that he was free for ever 'above the clouds'.

Margaret and John Evans

IAN

We had decided to be adventurous and have a family holiday abroad. This year we used a firm that hired caravans already in place and we chose to visit Paris and Interlaken. We set off in May 1984 – John and me, Anne (nine), Marie (six and a half) and Ian (three and a half). The car was so full that we could hardly see the children and we had a very happy time, enjoyed Paris and travelled to Interlaken.

On Sunday, 3 June 1984 I woke up suddenly fairly early and found Ian looking down at me and smiling. I was very surprised and looked again and he gave me a beautiful smile but didn't say anything. I sat up and asked what was wrong but he just smiled at me again and climbed over me and snuggled up between John and me. Later we all got up and Sunday was 'hair washing day'. In the showers we could hear Ian protesting but at last that was over and we had breakfast. A typical English family we tried to eat outside but it was too cold and we ended up back in the caravan. Then we set off to an English-speaking church we had discovered earlier. Ian was really fidgety during the sermon although I hoped he would go off to sleep, as usual. Eventually I took him out and we sat in the car and he signed his name very proudly at the bottom of the postcards I had written earlier. As it was pretty obvious that he wasn't going to sleep I relented and we had a game of football. When the others joined us we had a picnic together.

We went on a funicular railway up the Harde. We had to stand and we were at the front watching the driver. The girls were interested in knowing the cost of everything in English money and I told them, ending with 'and Ian was free.' Ian was very annoyed at this and interjected 'No, I'm not, I'm free and a half.'

The day rolled on as a happy family day. We played on the swings at the top of the mountain and walked down the family footpath stopping to have drinks and crisps on the way down. I would sit and do a little to my tapestry (which I'd been doing on holiday for several years) and Ian would run back to me and say 'Can I do some knitting?' I'd reply 'It's not knitting – it's a tapestry. You can do some when we're home' and we'd all laugh at what was becoming a family joke. John and Ian were pretending to be real mountain walkers and acquired stout sticks to use as staffs. The path started to get steep and I suddenly realised that Anne, Marie and I were wearing sandals which were really not very suitable for walking. We went on very carefully, while Ian and John stayed behind answering Ian's call of nature. As they were catching up with us, Anne turned round and called back to them that Ian had left his stick behind. Ian of course wanted to go and fetch it, so John let go of his hand.

Suddenly I heard a shout and John pushed past us yelling 'Ian has fallen'. Anne went tearing off after him leaving Marie and me standing there feeling empty, confused and not really believing what had happened. We went back and couldn't see where an accident had happened because there was a fence. I felt disorientated and empty. I called out 'Ian, John, Anne' but everything seemed deserted. It was quite frightening and Marie held on to me closely. After a while a woman came down and it was obvious that we were upset about something. Unfortunately she couldn't speak English and I couldn't speak German. Eventually we communicated in French that I had lost my son. She disappeared and I didn't really know what to do. Eventually I decided the best thing would be for Marie and me to walk down to the bottom of the mountain. We set off and half an hour later the woman we'd met earlier appeared and told me she had raised the alarm. She then insisted that she would accompany Marie and me. Then we met a group of German students who had Anne with them. She was upset because she had got lost and hadn't found either John or Ian. She also held my hand tightly as we carried on down the mountain, firmly escorted by this formidable lady and now a group of students. I felt cold inside and didn't know what to believe. It was like a nightmare. Eventually we reached the bottom of the mountain and there seemed to be loads of people there, including a policeman and two police cars. I was shown into one of the cars and this woman took Anne and Marie away from me. I became very upset and it was so difficult not being able to communicate with her and in the end I grabbed the girls who by then were crying and wanting to be with me. It was awful. The policeman intervened and spoke to the woman and Anne and Marie came in the car with me. We were driven to the police station and an officer who could speak some English went through my story. Communication was awful though. I couldn't understand what was happening and he certainly didn't understand all I said. After what seemed like hours John appeared with yet another policeman. Immediately it sounded like a shouting match. John speaks fluent German and everyone seemed so relieved that it appeared to me that everyone was suddenly speaking at the same time. I was feeling sick by then so I crept out with Anne and Marie to a coffee shop outside and sat in the fresh air. Everyone was looking up and the proprietor told me that the rescue helicopter had just gone up. I dissolved into tears and told her my son had fallen. From then on everything was a blur. Cups of coffee appeared, glasses of coke, fresh pastries, bars of chocolate . . . she couldn't do too much for us. The nightmare went on – I was totally disorientated and didn't really get a chance to talk to John. Eventually the helicopter pilot walked in, still in his flying clothes, and I knew by his face that Ian had died.

When we got back to the caravan I found out from John that he had scrambled off the path through the steeply sloping wooded mountainside trying to find Ian and had on more than one occasion slipped and lost his footing, dropping his glasses several times. It shocked me how easily I could have also lost John.

The Swiss authorities are very strict and on the Monday John was taken back to the scene of the fall and we were told that we couldn't leave the country until the authorities were satisfied and that there would be a meeting shortly. I spent the morning with Anne and Marie who wrote in their diaries their memories of Ian. We cried and laughed together as we wrote down his favourite sayings and which toys were special to him. My Swiss pen-friend came to see me in the afternoon. She had lost a baby from a cot death some years before and was extremely helpful to us in explaining the funeral director's procedures. She encouraged me to select Ian's favourite clothes to take to them. We also took his favourite toy – a car and caravan. She organised my sister Pat's travel within Switzerland. Pat had never even been abroad and she obtained a passport on the Monday morning and was with us by the evening. Our parents willingly volunteered to look after her two small boys so she contacted the school explaining the arrangements and left a note to her husband saying 'Gone to Switzerland'! She travelled Club Class and I'm sure she still believes that that is the normal way to fly! It was good to be together and we were five in number again. On Tuesday we were told that we could see Ian. I wasn't sure if I wanted to but when we got there I couldn't stop myself going in and he looked so lovely. He was wearing his own clothes, a blue jumper and trousers, his car and caravan were by his hands, and white lilac was all around his face. White lilac has become very precious to us now and we now have two bushes in our garden.

The authorities told us that we were free to leave the country and we left on the Wednesday, which was our wedding anniversary. Before leaving we posted the cards which Ian had so painstakingly signed and we learned later that it had really upset some people to receive them but I felt determined to send them. We also visited the café opposite the police station and they gave us a lovely box of Swiss chocolates. Pat made us have wine with our evening meal and instead of celebrating our anniversary, we shared our special memories of Ian. We each chose a special memory and toasted each one. Anne and Marie were very much part of this and in my recollections it was a very special evening – happy rather than overwhelmingly sad.

The rest of the trip back and all that happened is now a blur. There was surprisingly a lot of laughter. Each evening we rang John's mother who acted as a point of contact for all enquiries. She arranged the funeral with our vicar and took over all the responsibility for everything that needed doing in this country. In a funny way we felt isolated and cocooned in a sort of time warp which was safe and comforting. When I walked back into my home I was overwhelmed. My friend and neighbour, Angie, had sorted the post into two lots – sympathy and business – and had arranged flowers from our garden in each room. The house seemed to wrap itself around me and I felt properly at home. We had been thinking of moving but that idea just went away.

Pat helped me to clear away all of Ian's toys and clothes. She said I shouldn't throw anything away quickly in case I regretted it later so we bundled everything up and put it all away in boxes in the roof. Ian was the fifth of the grandchildren and had somehow acquired everything that the others were ready to pass on. He had twenty boxes of things to go away and was only three and a half. Anne had had her own room but started climbing into Ian's bunk bed which was under Marie's bed. I also found it so hard to go in that room so we bought new beds for the girls and let them share a room again. Somehow we felt that it was healthier for everyone.

My memory of the next few weeks is now hazy. Our vicar recommended that we hold the funeral service and the Thanksgiving Service on the same day as it would be too traumatic to go through it twice. Ian's funeral was held some fifty miles away and he was buried in a family grave. I remember Anne crying hysterically and almost falling into the hole when Ian was being lowered into the grave (and that was after all our arrangements for someone to take Anne and Marie for a walk during the committal). There was then a great rush to get back to Ian's Thanksgiving Service and we were fifteen minutes late! Anne was even later as she was in a car with her grandparents and some friends and they started off in the wrong direction. I got very worried and didn't want the service to begin until they had arrived. Apparently it was quite funny to watch everyone who had come from the funeral service because they all walked in at the back of the church and headed directly to the cloakrooms – a long procession of them! Our pianist was starting to wonder how much longer she'd have to improvise. The church was absolutely packed and everywhere I looked there were friends. It was wonderful and we felt so supported. I held my nephew's hand so hard that he had bruises on it afterwards. This service was made up of Ian's favourite hymns and choruses. His favourite was 'If you want to be great in God's kingdom'. This was a family joke because I have white hair and Ian used to sing 'If you want to be grey in God's kingdom' and laugh at me. I can't sing that song now. The church had arranged tea and refreshments in our home and I felt as if I were holding court because there were so many people there all caring deeply for us. In a way I didn't feel as if I were really there and I am sure that I was in shock.

My faith was very strong and particularly while travelling back to England I was totally dependent on my prayer life. I wasn't strong enough to do anything in my own strength and definitely experienced God's wrapping me round in feathers and comforting me with his tender care. It was a very real experience and although over the last ten years my faith has wavered (sometimes very badly) I can't just ignore my experience then. In a way it was as if God removed a layer and came close to me and I was able to see him which I haven't been able to do since. I remember feeling very strongly that if I could telephone Ian and find out that he was all right that I would be able to cope. I wondered about silly things such as if he was changing his underwear!

I was very lucky with my friends – they were all so thoughtful and kind. Someone seemed to be there whenever I needed them. I hadn't been alone in the house for nearly ten years – I had always had a toddler around me and suddenly to have all this time without being prepared for it was very difficult. The hardest times were shopping, because everyone else seemed to have children with them, and being in the kitchen, as I had always had a little 'helper' there in the past. Another friend left her own little boy at nursery and visited me and persuaded me to help her make cakes or whatever in my kitchen rather than just sitting and drinking coffee. It took me a while to realise that this was her strategy – at first I thought that she was extremely busy and couldn't visit me without cooking at the same time! My mother-in-law bought us a microwave to help this aversion to the kitchen which helped a bit. Immediately after Ian's funeral I helped at the girls' school as a dinner lady for several weeks as they were desperate and at that time I was too weak-willed to say no. I found having somewhere to go each day very constructive and the children refreshing. They weren't afraid to ask me questions and their interest was helpful. My very close neighbour had one day off a week and she gave me that time. We went out every Wednesday and sometimes shopped, sometimes visited museums and started researching our family trees. Her greatest gift to me was the time she gave me. I also spent money – it was a difficult time and for many years with small children I hadn't had many clothes and suddenly it became important to me that I owned new clothes. Financially I put a great deal of pressure on our family.

Anne showed her emotions quite easily and cried at school when hymns mentioned mountains. She had a very good schoolteacher who was a family friend and kept a close eye on her. Marie found it much harder to show her emotions. Her teacher at that time was very strict. It would have been difficult to pull the wool over her eyes, yet several times the school rang and I had to collect Marie who was not well. When Marie came home she always seemed fine, but on each of these occasions I had been in the middle of a deep weeping session. It was almost as if she sensed that I needed her. She was always deeply welcome and helped me to cope. She had two special friends who actually fought over who would look after her. It started at the Thanksgiving Service and continued throughout her Primary and Junior schooling.

The British inquest was held in August. It went reasonably well and I realised that I had been terrified in case it was decided that we had been at fault for being on this particular walk. In fact an English policeman had been to Switzerland and examined the files and he reported that there were no problems with children using the path. It was also reported that Ian had been wearing suitable footwear, and also that he must have died instantly. Apart from the problems of journalists wanting to question us I had a definite feeling of relief when the inquest was over.

John was working in London at that time and left the home in the mornings about 6.30 and didn't get back till 7 or later so I had long days. In many ways I felt that I was luckier than him with the support I was given and, of course, I still had to feed Anne and Marie and take them to Brownies, swimming, etc. I remember one very bad day when I had been shopping and it seemed that everyone had tiny children with them asking for biscuits and chattering on. I made it to the till and drove home crying. I got inside my own home and felt safe and let out a howl – the sort that you would only do on your own and the sort of howl you only make when you have lost someone. There was a clattering upstairs and my friend's sixteen-year-old son came down. He had been painting our bathroom ceiling during the school holidays and I hadn't realised that he was coming that day. I felt so awful but he was kindness itself and made me a cup of coffee and tried to make me talk. Surprisingly he wasn't embarrassed – more concerned. Some days before I had been given the name of The Compassionate Friends but hadn't wanted to contact them, but after this episode I thought it would be good to do so.

There wasn't a meeting held in Berkshire but a kind woman was always available to listen to me and wrote letters. I found it so comforting to speak to someone who *knew* what I was feeling. She was always available and often rang me to find out how I was getting on and she always seemed to tune in to me on days when I was feeling very low. There came a time when I felt very guilty if some hours elapsed when I forgot to think about Ian and it was so good to be reassured that this was a normal feeling. Reflecting on these feelings now it is difficult to work out why our telephone calls helped me so much but I can still remember the relief I felt when we spoke and she understood what I was trying to say. I am convinced that I would have ended up at the doctor's surgery asking for help in the form of tablets or counselling. As it was my eczema and colitis (which I suffered from badly in my teens) became quite difficult problems. My husband had a growth in his chest a year later which had to be removed. Fortunately this was benign but I wonder if it was a reaction to the stress he was under. He had to take two months off work.

While standing on the mountain with Marie I had felt helpless not being able to communicate with anyone. After the accident I often thought about that time when the only way I could make the German lady understand me was to mime the accident. John encouraged me to learn German and I went to weekly classes and even though I am not fluent now I could certainly make myself understood in an emergency again.

We have always 'celebrated' Ian's birthday and anniversary of death. In fact it has become a family excuse to do something different. We always share a 'special' meal and have also been to shows in the West End or other evenings out. If we want to go somewhere different we often say 'Let's go on Ian's birthday'. I often think that friends think it is morbid but it is our way of handling our emotions and it seems to work for us.

Several years later we needed to clear our roof. Pat came and spent a day helping to sort through Ian's belongings. It was a day of laughter and tears. As so many of the clothes and toys had originally belonged to her sons it was also a moving time for her. We were able to distance ourselves and realise that a lot of his clothes really had seen better days and throw them out. Others went to charity shops so we went out on a delivery round – somehow I felt too embarrassed to take everything to one shop. We also sorted out lots of cars and toys and took them round to John's young godchild. At the end of this day both Pat and I were emotionally drained, had violent headaches and were quite grubby but felt that we had moved on in our grieving.

This year was the tenth anniversary of Ian's death and our life has continued to change. John rarely finishes work before 7 in the evenings, although he no longer works in London. I work full-time, Anne is at university and Marie has just done her GCSEs. We decided that apart from a meal out we wouldn't do anything special. Anne came home for the weekend a day early which was nice, although I was somewhat sceptical that her lectures were cancelled for the Friday. John got up at six as normal and came rushing in to me saying what was this all about. As I was asleep I wasn't very coherent and had no idea what he was talking about. There was a notice pinned up on the mirror in the bathroom saying 'Your presence is not required at work today' in Anne's writing. I woke up fairly rapidly and still had no idea of what was going on. It seemed a rather cruel joke to play which was not like Anne and it wasn't April Fool's Day. Eventually we woke Anne to find out about it. She said she had been in touch with John's manager and my boss and we were both given a day off. John and I sat stunned and didn't really know what to do – after all it was still only just after six in the morning. Eventually John decided not to go to work but said he would ring in at work at about eight. He had thought his manager was on leave that day! I went in to work at eight (I'd left my desk in a dreadful mess) and also rang my boss at eight. Both John and I were told firmly we had the day off which left us speechless. Anne and Marie had organised this day for us as a special celebration because of the year.

It was a day that got better and better. We had coffee in a place I'd always wanted to visit and then we went down to Ian's grave which needed some tidying up. Anne and Marie produced a floral Teddy Bear from the back of the car which they had collected

and hidden. John and I have never been in the habit of buying
large wreaths and we were overwhelmed. We spent a pleasant
afternoon pottering around Petersfield and neither of the girls
argued. We drove back to Reading and went out for a Chinese
meal. We shared a lot of memories and Anne said she had been in
touch with the school teacher who had been with her when Ian
died. She is studying for a nursing degree and had been researching child bereavement and what was done in school. This had
made her want to find out more clearly about her own experience
as so much time had passed since Ian died. While doing her
research she had used the SIBBS (see pg 204) newsletter a great
deal and read fairly widely. John and I were amazed that all this
had happened without our being aware and listening to both
Anne and Marie gave us quite a lot of insight into their feelings.
Both of them had felt a lot of resentment that they had not been
allowed to say goodbye to Ian and see him after he had died. We
had been trying to protect them and had never realised how upset
they were at being excluded. John also felt resentful because he
had given a great deal of information to the Swiss authorities and
signed the statement, but had not been allowed to keep a copy of
it. I had never known about the resentment they all felt. The girls
had found a photograph which was good of Ian, but not of the
child he was sitting next to. They had had it rephotographed and
blown up focusing on Ian and they presented it to us at the meal.
I was nearly in tears but the wonderful day still wasn't finished
because Anne and Marie insisted on paying for the meal (a first
ever!) and when we got home a beautiful bouquet of flowers had
been delivered to us. It really was a day that instead of being sad
with painful memories became almost triumphal in its pleasure
and very, very special.

The past ten years have made me grow as a person. I have
become much more aware of unhappiness around me and seem
to be able to pick up unhappy vibrations. It's as if people who are
grieving for some loss feel that I can relate to their grief and I do
find I am able to 'hear' what they are saying. I have also been so

touched by a great deal of kindness shown to us and to me in particular, often from people who have not been particularly close. In recent years I have valued friendships I have made through The Compassionate Friends because there is always a base to build upon. Material 'things' seem very important at the time and certainly oil the wheels, but ultimately are they really that important? Invisible things such as friendship and relationships are very much more important. Our family is a particularly close one and I always feel that John, Anne and Marie are very protective of me. The death of Ian has been a learning experience and I am just very grateful that we shared his life for three and a half years.

Pam, John, Anne and Marie Scoble

THERESE

Looking at the lovely child in my arms on 28 December 1934, there was no way I could foresee the years of unhappiness in store for her.

Therese grew up in peaceful and idyllic surroundings; my husband was a gardener on country estates. She had everything to make her life a success, everything to live for. She had a good brain and was the dux of her class at school. Languages were no problem to her – she was fluent in French and scored 90 per cent in her Latin exams. She was also very clever with her hands. Embroidery, knitting, cooking – she excelled in them all.

She was a very loving and caring person until, at the age of twenty-two, she met and fell under the spell of the man who was later to be her husband. From then on her life, and mine, was to remain a continual source of unhappiness. He destroyed wedding presents from her friends and family, breaking her wedding china and throwing out other gifts. She tried to keep it all a secret. When asked about bruises on her legs, she said she had fallen in the coalhouse. I tried to speak to his mother, but she said my daughter's black eyes were caused by an accident with his ring.

A few months after marrying she was pushed downstairs, which resulted in a miscarriage. It was then that she decided to come home and give herself time to think about what to do about the future. A recorded letter arrived from her husband, saying that he was going to South Africa and pointing out that as a wife, it was her duty to go with him. Consulting a lawyer, she was advised that if he went she could get a divorce on the grounds of separation, but at that time it was very difficult.

His mother, knowing her movements, waylaid my daughter on

her way from work and, managing to put on a great act, told her how her son only wanted to go to South Africa so that he could give her a much better life. She came pleading and cajoling on his behalf, telling her how he would settle down, how two years' conscription had unsettled him, how he would get a good job and more money there. Any ill treatment was apparently because of the uncertainty and all that was needed was for the relationship to be permanent. However, his mother was every bit as keen to see him go as she was finding it increasingly difficult to explain the bruises. They couldn't all be put down to accidents.

My daughter returned to her husband. I remember his terribly piercing eyes. Perhaps he hypnotised her; certainly he had an incomprehensible hold over her. I think, even then, he threatened to kill her.

So that we, her parents, could not make contact with her, he beat her into agreeing to go to South Africa with him. As they had to stay with his brother in Cape Town I wrote to him expressing my anxiety with regard to her safety. He was the very opposite to his mother. He assured me that no harm would befall Therese. It was with a great sense of relief that I read those words and I felt that everything was now going to be all right.

My relief was short-lived. When her husband found out that he could not continue his sadism, he left for Johannesburg. She travelled up a short time later on a cheap fare. I don't know the reason, but by the time she reached her destination, she wrote to say she was feeling very ill.

She returned to Scotland for the birth of her first child. The cablegram we sent to him to announce the birth was returned undelivered. The house was unoccupied. It was five or six weeks before she received any correspondence – he would disappear for periods – yet still she returned to South Africa.

The promises his mother made on his behalf, about a better life in South Africa, were all a load of rubbish. The ill treatment did not stop and Therese had to support herself all her married life. When her children were too small for her to work away from home she did home catering, baking wedding cakes. Her business was very successful. No one would have guessed at her private misery.

Looking back at all the years of worry and wondering why she didn't leave him, it became apparent she knew he would kill her which, in fact, is what he did. His family in Scotland protected him to the last. Two members of his family came to tell us that our daughter and her husband had both been killed in a car crash. We were reeling with shock at the news, but none of us – not my husband, nor my other children – believed what we had been told. We were desperate for news; we wanted to know what had happened to Therese all those miles away from home, but we had great difficulty in finding out the true nature of her death.

Not having a telephone at that time made it very difficult to make contact. We barely knew how to use a public telephone, and when we did get through my head was pounding so hard and I was trembling so much that I couldn't understand what was being said.

I had to avail myself of friends' forbearance – asking strangers about my daughter's death, phoning from neighbours' houses, but more often than not finding out nothing.

We enquired for information at the South African Embassy, but they couldn't give us any details. Writing to the police in South Africa for the result of the inquest, we were told to contact the immediate family. In my state of shock it never occurred to me that her grown-up family would be next of kin and that I, her mother, would not be entitled to information. I began to realise how great the distance between us really was, but the years and the miles didn't make her any less my daughter.

We wrote to her family, but again, no answer. Eventually I remembered the brother in South Africa, the only member of that family who had ever seemed to understand. The most obvious contact, but the one I had overlooked in my panic and shock. At last I heard the truth.

I found out that my daughter's husband had been deported

from South Africa some time ago – his brother used the word 'depravity' but gave no more details. Therese, he told us, had been trying to start a new life. No one knows how her husband had managed to return to South Africa, but the official inquest from the South African police filled us with horror. The bodies of my daughter and her husband were found by the police in the burned-out wreck of a car. Apparently he abducted his ex-wife (my daughter) from her home, the abduction being reported to the police. It is extremely difficult to establish exactly what transpired next. The court's finding was that 'the death of [Therese] was probably caused by her husband who then committed suicide' (Commissioner, South African police).

I was not surprised. For over twenty years I had walked the floor in the dead of night, crying and expecting something like this to happen. It was, I believe, a murder in waiting. The fear had been lingering at the back of my mind all those years. My God, I had often wondered, what was she putting up with now? Now I felt as if I would never sleep again – indeed, to this day I still suffer from insomnia.

My husband had just come out of intensive care having partly recovered from a severe heart attack. In view of my husband's condition I could not tell him the true story, which made the burden that much heavier for me to bear. As a matter of fact, he died never knowing the details of her murder.

My first reaction was bitterness and anger towards my daughter. How could anyone so clever be so stupid? My husband always told me never to interfere, but I remembered that before she married I urged her to think carefully. Could she manage him? Why hadn't she listened? Why didn't she stay in Scotland where her family could have helped? On sleepless nights I would go over it all again, feeling dizzy, my head aching, trying to find something I could have said or done to alter the outcome. I carried my bitterness through to his family. Even now I have a strong dislike of anyone bearing his name.

I discovered that his family in Scotland had not told his mother the truth because of her age. They had wanted to protect her. That filled me with rage. It seemed so very unfair. There was no one to protect me from that awful truth; and the real culprit, her son, was already dead, beyond the reach of justice. Had it happened in this country everyone would have known. His memory would have been publicly shamed. Perhaps that was why I needed to tell everyone what had happened. I told everybody I met. Maybe I thought that by telling people I could rid myself of the pain. Maybe I just wanted everyone to share my grief. People who had known Therese still stopped to ask how she was keeping, and I would tell them quite bluntly that she had been murdered. It felt like I was hitting back.

However, it was really painful to watch their discomfort and embarrassment. I ended up feeling more sorry for them than for myself. Most people would be shocked and would hurry away. They could think of nothing to say. One woman who had known my daughter and her husband said it was because he really loved her. I cannot accept that love had any part in what happened.

When Therese's family were small they had come home for one visit. The children had seemed very subdued and evasive; very careful how they answered any questions. Only once, her son, who was then only six, said he would like to beat his father with a belt. That was almost twenty years ago. I've had no contact with my grandchildren in South Africa since their mother died – no more letters, no news. In my grief I tried to blot their name from my memory because it was the name of their father. I have a sense of guilt about that because I have nothing against the children. They, themselves, deserved no part of the unhappiness. Much later I learned that they had also rejected their father, refusing to bury his body. For me the most unfortunate part of the whole sorry affair is that I have lost out on my grandchildren – are there now great-grandchildren?

In many ways my grief had been spent over the years I had lived in dread of something like this happening. I also think my anger helped carry me through at first.

My husband and I were both over seventy when my daughter died. We had lived a long time and together we had coped with all the bad times in our lives. I had to think of him now and nurse him back to health. Not being able to talk to him about what had happened also helped me to block out the horrific manner of Therese's death. Even now I refuse to dwell on that.

I had always taken a pride in my appearance and I remember how I used to put on my lipstick with trembling hands and try and cover the blotches around my eyes with extra make-up. I never wore black. I forced myself to keep going.

Although we did not consider ourselves old, my husband and I had reached an age when life was very precious to us. When we felt down it was easy to remind ourselves of how lucky we were – my husband was making a full recovery and in years to come we were to celebrate our diamond wedding anniversary. Many of our friends had died, or were in poor health. We also had a close-knit family in Scotland and the ups and downs of their lives helped us cope with Therese's death.

Having spent all my life living in the country I was also more attuned to the various changes in nature which teach you to accept things that cannot change. I had always been a keen gardener and the various colours of the seasons gave me a great deal of pleasure and a feeling of peace. They made me aware that, whatever destiny dealt you, it was better to accept and rise above it.

When my children left home I had to accept that I was no longer the most important person in their lives; that they would make their own decisions and their own way in the world. It did not stop me wanting to be there, or worrying about them, but I was no longer allowed the same involvement. In a way, I lost them all when they left home.

With Therese, because of the distance and circumstances, the loss had always been a particularly painful one, but the link had been broken. Now I had to accept her death as the final step in our separation. With a sore heart I had to stand aside and let others, closer to her now than I had been for years, take charge and mourn her. I comforted myself with the thought that I had known her when she was young and happy. In the company of my grandchildren in Scotland, I again found that pleasure. They are a continual source of comfort to me, bringing a sense of healing.

Being a housewife, I had always been quite content looking after my family, but when I felt myself becoming a prisoner of my own misery I got out more, meeting people, making new friends.

I learned to drive (though no longer a young woman!), thus enabling me to take my grandchildren and great-grandchildren to the seaside. At that time the sea was the main attraction. The beaches were always crowded and to see the children enjoying themselves did much to bring me back to normality.

Nearing the age of eighty-five, I can say that time is a great healer. The memory does linger on and there are still moments of sadness, regret and loss. Now that my great-grandchildren are growing I cannot, at times, but wonder what may lie ahead for them.

However, I also have a deep sense of peace. There will come a day when all this sadness will be rewarded. We must keep faith and believe that some day we will be reunited.

We owe that to our loved ones.

Margaret Gladstone

LISA

'Ate logo' is Portuguese for 'See you soon'. It is the parting gesture between family and friends in Brazil. We picked up the habit of saying it too while living in Rio de Janeiro. We had moved to Brazil when my husband Dave, a geologist for a major oil company, was posted there. When we moved in early 1981 Lisa was about sixteen months old. Kevin was born there on 26th November that year.

For most of our stay in Rio we enjoyed ourselves. We loved the local people and they were generally very friendly. Rio conjures up all sorts of romantic notions and we have many treasured memories. However, our life there was tragically altered, when our beautiful little daughter, Lisa, died from drowning in a friend's swimming pool. She was three years old. 'Ate logo' forms part of the epitaph on her headstone. We often said it to Lisa each night before she went to sleep. We felt it was very apt because one day we hope to be reunited with her.

Lisa and I had gone to a friend's house so our children could play together as they had many times before. We left the two children to play in the garden while we had tea. To this day I do not know what made Lisa go to the pool in the garden. She had never done so previously, without supervision, and we had no reason to suspect she would that particular day, especially since we'd given them a child's paddling pool to splash about in. Inexcusably, for once, to my eternal regret, I forgot the unpredictability of children.

When we found her in the pool we got her out as quickly as we could. We tried to revive her but couldn't, so we rushed her to a nearby health centre. The doctors took over immediately; they tried all means possible to resuscitate Lisa, but alas to no avail.

While we were struggling to save her in the garden I prayed to God to give her back to me. When I knew it was too late I prayed again to Him to somehow give me the strength I would need to cope with my life without my precious little Lisa.

The death of one of your children is the ultimate pain of any parent. In our relatively healthy country it is something we never contemplate. I was the same until Lisa's death. Of course, I was horrified and saddened on hearing of a child's death, whether it was through illness, accident or, much worse, murder. However, it did not affect me, so my life continued unabated.

The day after Lisa's death we were allowed to take her back home to Glasgow, in Scotland, for burial. The nature of Dave's job meant we could be moved from country to country, making it difficult for us to visit her grave. We knew we would always be naturally drawn to our home town so it was very important to us that Lisa should be laid to rest there. About six weeks after her funeral we returned to Rio.

Initially what helped me was just being allowed to talk about Lisa. I don't know why, but I found myself repeating over and over the details of the accident. I was lucky to have a number of friends who were willing to listen to me. We were so far away from home that I depended on my friends a great deal and will always be thankful to them. As time dragged on I became worried that they would stop coming to see me and I started to bottle things up. Eventually, one night, I was inconsolable. I was really in despair, then a thought came to me. Since I couldn't speak about my feelings, why not write them down? So I did.

Soon after returning to Brazil I decided to get back into the routine I had before the accident. I needed to have some structure to my day and I still had Kevin. As much as I could have shut myself away from the world, he still needed playmates, even more than ever. He couldn't understand what had happened to Lisa, but it was clear that he missed her too.

While we were home in Scotland for the funeral we were given the opportunity of remaining there instead of returning to Brazil.

We were told that if we did not go back all our belongings would be packed up for us and shipped home. We decided to return because we felt that we could cope with going back. We, ourselves, were coping as well as could be expected under the circumstances. However, although most of our friends were very supportive, there were those who would not, or could not, accept the way I was dealing with my loss. They assumed that, because I was getting back into my former routines and beginning to pick up the threads of my torn life, I was somehow not facing facts. They thought I was shutting it all away in the back of my mind, only for it to rear its head some day in the future. What they didn't see was me collapsed in a chair at the end of a day from the sheer effort of putting on a brave face for Kevin's sake, to ensure that his little world wasn't any more disrupted than it had already been.

I found this pressure to conform to someone else's belief about how to cope with bereavement too much to bear. I had more than enough to cope with as it was. This made us decide to accept an offer to return to Scotland. Dave was given a job in the company's Aberdeen office. We bought a house in Inverurie where we'd lived prior to going to Brazil. This unassuming little town in the north-east of Scotland is where my healing truly first began. I could retreat into the quietness of the rural lifestyle and still have enough friends around for support. Yet I could also be anonymous insofar as I could grieve at my own pace. We have to allow each person to grieve in their own, individual way because our different backgrounds and upbringings do make a difference to the way we come to terms with this greatest of all losses.

Later on in my bereavement I found that my moods instead of steadily improving, would go up and down. I used the television to escape. It didn't make me forget my pain, it simply gave my mind some kind of distractions, otherwise I might have gone mad. It was on an afternoon while I was watching *Pebble Mill* that I first heard of The Compassionate Friends. I jotted down the address, but it was some months later before I contacted them. Thank heavens I did.

However, what did help me, and still does sustain me, was my faith: the belief I have held on to right from the start that God would give me the strength and the willpower to learn to live without my little Lisa. Yes, there have been times when I have thought I could not go on, but He hasn't let me down. It is my own doubting of myself which makes me falter.

The irony of my situation, as may be the case in others, was my immediate family, who did not talk of Lisa's death. Of course, in the days following her death they did, but later on, and even now, I feel they think it will upset me too much to do so. In reality I believe it is their own pain they fear more. Friends were easier. On first encounter with friends I would deliberately mention Lisa by name. This cleared the air and let them know it was all right to recall memories they might otherwise have avoided for fear of bringing Lisa to mind. I didn't go on at length about her; just a brief reference was enough. At first I wasn't too aware of people who didn't want to talk of Lisa. I guess my need to talk was so strong I was oblivious to others' reluctance to listen. As my loss did not happen locally many people in Inverurie did not know of it, therefore it was only as I got to know my neighbours that I came across a mix of reactions, some people wanting to know more and others who were not interested.

I would advise parents to keep photographs of their children on show. It is painful at first, but you will, in the long run, find it easier to look at them and remember happier times. After all, if you lose a parent, or grandparent, you wouldn't take their pictures off the wall, would you?

I have quite a practical nature. I knew it was pointless to hold on to many of Lisa's toys. I was aware that Kevin could use some of them, but the others I donated to charity. Her clothes I gave to a friend who I knew would put them to good use. I didn't want to just throw them away. I made myself use her plastic toddler cups and plates with Kevin, as nothing would have been gained by throwing them away or by refusing to use them. Even now we still have games and jigsaws of Lisa's which my other three chil-

dren have had pleasure from. Far from upsetting me, they allow
me an opportunity to tell them about their sister because, even
though Fiona and Mark never knew Lisa, and Kevin can barely
remember her, I feel it is important that they know who the girl in
the photos is.

As Lisa died in February her birthday, being in November, was
far enough away for me to assume that by then I would have
come to terms with her loss. However, the nearer it drew, the
more anxious I became. I had no idea how I would cope nor how
to prepare myself for her birthdate on the 7th. As it turned out,
my worry was worse than the actual day itself. I was surprised
that I didn't feel as bad as I thought I should. Subsequent birthdays have been varied. Sometimes I go to a church somewhere or
find a quiet place where I can be alone with my thoughts. Some
I've barely dwelt upon, others have been more traumatic. Those
are the ones that are milestones – for example, her fifth and tenth
and, most recently, her first teenage birthday, her thirteenth.

The first Christmas was doubly hard for Dave, whose father
died the same year. That was therefore a particularly quiet occasion. We still had Kevin, of course, and we could not deny him
his Christmas treats, so we did what we could on his behalf, but
the rest of the time we lost ourselves in television. I expect we
were all actually deep in thought, but couldn't share the depth of
our feelings with each other.

Again, as the first anniversary approached, I was filled with
anxiety as to how I would cope. Once more the days leading up
to it proved to be more harrowing than the day itself. I think this
is because you become so worried and build yourself into such a
state that it turns out to be an anticlimax. Like Lisa's birthdays,
her anniversaries have varied in intensity, depending on my
frame of mind as they occurred.

I think the initial strains were caused by a lack of understanding between Dave and myself. This was when I could see that our
different upbringings made a difference to the way we
approached our loss. Perhaps it was the gender factor, but what

was clear was that we were not dealing with it in the same way. This made me feel that Dave did not feel the loss as much as I did. I was making the same mistake as many mothers do, believing that fathers do not experience the same depths of bereavement. I know this is wrong. Men do have different ways of dealing with feelings. This does not make their problems any easier to solve. It might, in some ways, be more difficult for them to resolve their tangled emotions which mothers are more freely permitted to show within society as a whole.

Once I accepted that Dave had the right to grieve in his own way, just as I demanded to, the strains began to lift, so we learned to know when to grieve alone and when to grieve together. I did get angry, although it took me a while to recognise the anger as part of my coming to terms. I would feel a build-up of tension inside me, then I would snap at Dave or Kevin. I felt I had no right to be angry and that being thus I was showing a lack of belief in God's faith in me. Then I came to understand that I did have a right to feel this emotion. Though I was angry at the situation I was in, I didn't know what I had done to deserve it. Why should I have to endure such pain? Why me? I did not blame God for bringing this tragedy down on me as some form of punishment. I do not believe he is a cruel God, but a loving Father. I cannot pinpoint a moment when I can say my anger subsided. I think, like many of the emotions we experience, it gradually diminishes in intensity, but never leaves you completely. There seem to be various times when these very raw feelings are stirred up once more.

It is now over eleven years since Lisa died. My feelings, of course, are not quite as sensitive as they were initially, but I don't have to think too deeply to feel the intense longing of any bereaved parent. I feel guilty although Dave has never blamed me or even suggested in any way that I was responsible for Lisa's death. I accept that there was not a lot I could have done at the time. However, since I was the one with her, I feel I should have been more aware of the danger the swimming pool presented. I know, like many other people, I assumed such tragedies happened to others, but not to me. I guess I got over these feelings of guilt by understanding that even if I'd been aware of Lisa being in the water, the outcome would have been the same. She had simply been in the water too long. Dave's refusal to impart any blame on me has helped me to resolve the guilt for the most part.

I was helped a lot by both talking and writing to bereaved parents. Though I never asked for help myself, I was aware that I was being helped by extending help to others. When I had established a connection with The Compassionate Friends' Glasgow branch I was put in touch with bereaved parents in the Aberdeen area. Eventually we met as a group, once a month, in one member's house. It helped a great deal just to know what we were feeling was quite normal. We also had the freedom to talk about our dead children instead of meeting that glazed look at the mere mention of their names. Far from being morbid, these groups were quite light-hearted. There were times, of course, when some of us might be close to tears, but it was all right because we all understood. No one there was afraid to cry.

I know it's not easy to walk into a room full of strangers, but that room full of strangers could be the saving of you because what you receive is a compassionate welcome. None of us wants to be there, but we are there for each other. It is very difficult to explain to a newly bereaved parent that things will get better. You can only assure them that, given time, they will be able to come to terms with their loss and reassure them that they will never forget their child, which is a common worry. Just because society has put your loss down as another statistic doesn't mean you have to as well. They should be kind to themselves and not expect too much too soon. Their loss is not like the loss of a grandparent, or parent, and should not therefore be treated in the same way.

I was at a Compassionate Friends house group, about two and a half years after Lisa's death, when one of the group mentioned that we should try to be more positive about life. We discussed the fact that out children's lives were something we should be happy about. Yes, we did have the right to be sad at their loss, but couldn't we be happy for having known them? We agreed that it was all right, despite our inner sadness, to allow ourselves some happy times. We felt that our children, whether they were able to witness our grief or not, would not wish us only sadness and pain from their existence. Even though the pain of Lisa's loss will always be with me, it is worth it for having had her share in at least part of my life.

The sense of feeling positive about life is not something that came spontaneously to me. It was more a gradual process of going forward, overcoming one hurdle to be faced with yet another you hadn't bargained for. However, having faced and overcome many hurdles, I feel much more contented than I ever imagined could be possible from a situation such as mine. I would say time helps rather than heals. Initially you believe, as most people do, that after six or seven weeks things will start to get back to normal. When they don't, that is when you worry whether you are normal or not. Time hangs heavy in the early days of bereavement and each minute seems an eternity, but very slowly it moves on and eventually you accept the situation and are able to live a more positive life.

For my part, because Lisa was only three years old when we lost her, I had this terrible fear that everyone would forget she ever existed. 'Why should they remember her?' I thought. She hadn't had time to make her mark. That is when I decided to write; not necessarily about her death so much as about how her life had influenced me. How, through having known her, my life has been enriched and has become more meaningful, despite her short time with me.

Fortunately for Kevin, early on in my grief I realised that my sadness was affecting him. Whenever I cried in his company he would ask why I was crying. I would try to explain that it was because Lisa couldn't be with us. I thought it was right that he should be shielded from normal emotional reactions. Then I noticed that on one particular day when I was crying, he was saddened by my tears. I knew I had to attempt, at least, to be stronger for Kevin's benefit. I still didn't totally protect him from my 'down' patches, but I learned to hold back the tears, at least some of the time. He was too young, at fourteen months, to understand what had happened to Lisa, or where she was. I didn't attempt to explain, but now, whenever any of the children ask about her, I am quite happy to answer their questions. They have not yet asked about her actual death. Time will tell if they do. When they do I will be as open about it as possible.

Mark, our younger son, was born two years later on 2 February 1985. At that time I did not feel I could cope emotionally with a daughter, so I was delighted when he was born. In many ways he is very like Lisa in appearance and nature, but I am pleased to say I am happy about that. As the boys grew and were becoming less dependent on me, I would often wonder if I should try to have another daughter. Then I would tell myself to be content with my two healthy sons.

I began to consider what I should do with myself; should I get a job, return to education, or stay at home? Ever since Lisa's death I have found writing to be a great comfort. I find that once I have put my feelings down on paper I can cope better with them. So I decided to try to build a career as a writer. Then, in June 1989, I discovered I was pregnant. My emotions were very confused. Was I doing the right thing? Was I hoping too much for a girl? How would I react should I have another boy? Of course, I knew that when the baby was born I would love it whatever sex it happened to be.

On 3 February 1990 Fiona was born. My husband was there and when we saw we had another daughter we cried. Her birth just took us right back to the day Lisa was born. Our tears were a mixture of happiness and sadness. Sadness for the daughter we'd lost and happiness for the new daughter we had. Fiona is not a replacement for Lisa. She is a little treasure sent to help us through the hurt.

Another source of comfort has been, of course, my husband
Dave, ever there coping in his own way, putting his arms around
me whenever necessary. Kevin helped by being there for me to
look after and, moreover, to love and give me a purpose in
rebuilding my shattered world.

I would advise newly bereaved parents, despite their pain, not
to forget the ones they still have as they will be hurting too. It's
not their fault that their brother or sister has died. They should
not be expected to fill their sibling's place. Discuss your feelings
with them; if you can share with them they will be able to share
their hurt with someone too. They might not completely share
their feelings with you. They might turn to a teacher or a relative,
but that will be because they don't want to add to your pain. It is
up to the parents to be honest with their surviving children in the
hope that they will feel that they still have the right to go on living, even though their siblings cannot.

If you are still lucky enough to have children, as I am, then
you should be thankful for them. For those who do not, I can
only pray that you find solace for your own particular pain. No
one else can begin to understand unless they have experienced
the same degree of loss.

Even though it is quite a few years since we lost Lisa, I am only
now beginning to recall things we did together. I don't know if this
is usual or not. I suppose it could be linked to the fact that Fiona has
just passed the age that Lisa was when she died and that I am experiencing with her things I did, or might have done, with Lisa. It
might be that, until now, I wasn't strong enough to deal with real,
deep-seated memories. What I have noticed is that they seem to
come unbidden into my mind. Perhaps it is because of this anthol-
ogy that I am being made to go back and allow these memories to
be aired at last. Whatever it is I am glad, because I thought they had
gone for good and I am at long last achieving what I set out to do
over ten years ago: setting down on paper how I coped, with the
sole aim that, even if it helped just one other person, I would have
succeeded in doing something out of my love for Lisa.

My perspective on life has changed as a result of the death. I am more aware of life's effects on people. Not many people have a completely easy time of it; many people suffer in silence, when they needn't, as it often seems that society does not like to be burdened by tales of woe. This is why I am glad to see more self-help groups starting up. It is sad that they need to, but it is the best way to receive the level of understanding necessary for coping with the variety of ailments and problems life throws at people. Even if you feel these things are self-imposed or punishment from above, bereaved parents still need help, understanding and reassurance.

There are things that still throw me, such as if someone I know personally loses a child. However, I am a much stronger person than I was before.

What I would like to say to newly bereaved parents is that you should follow your own gut feelings. If it feels right for you, do it. It doesn't matter who understands the decisions you make regarding funerals or whatever. At the end of the day, if it helps you cope that little bit more, then so be it.

Betty Madill

KENNETH

and the start of The Compassionate Friends

On the morning of 21 May 1968 the children, Angela our daughter aged fourteen and Kenneth aged nearly twelve, prepared for school. In the way of families, last minute messages were thick in the air: 'I shall be late home, Mum, I'm at cricket training', 'I won't be in for tea, I'm going to a friend's'. They came, both of them, to kiss us goodbye. Kenneth had come round the back of the settee and, still talking to his mother, leaned over and kissed me. He jumped back in momentary embarrassment, we all laughed – he and I had stopped kissing as a form of affection, favouring now a handshake or a touch in the manner of men.

With the usual farewell calls they mounted their cycles and they set off in opposite directions to their schools. But Kenneth never reached his. At about 8.30 a.m. a small van cut the corner at the junction – the driver didn't see him.

The death of a twelve-year-old in the Coventry and Warwickshire Hospital was nothing novel: death of the young from illness, accident, suicide and even murder was part of the routine for a busy town centre hospital. For the ordinary, average family, it was something that happened to others, something you read or heard about and were no doubt saddened by – possibly sparing a brief thought for the family of the child.

And then the tragedy strikes you. It is *your* child lying there in the intensive care unit, listening to the admissions doctor's optimistic utterings: 'A simple skull fracture, I've seen worse.' But your own instinct tells you differently and it is soon confirmed by the consultant: your child, your beloved child, is going to die.

But what about those miraculous recoveries? Surely there is

still time? Surely the best brain surgeon in the world can get here, can save Kenneth, our son? But no, a short exploratory operation, the comparing of notes with some apparently eminent surgeon in Birmingham and suddenly there is no hope.

A young clergyman, the Revd Simon Stephens, assistant hospital chaplain, says a prayer over Kenneth's bed. There is another boy, Billy, who is dying of cancer; there's no hope for him either. We wonder how his mother and father are feeling. They've been here for six months, we're only on our third day and it's unbearable, yes unbearable, watching your child slowly die.

But God, what about God? He can do anything if He's a mind to. He's omnipotent. Surely he can save Kenneth and Billy? I offer a trade-off: I'll do anything to save Kenneth – anything! Take my life, I'll be a missionary, I'll give blood – anything! My wife Iris, Kenneth's mother, prays quietly: talking to him, calling him back, holding his hand in which is a small cross put there by the chaplain.

But God is not saving any children at the Coventry and Warwickshire Hopsital that day. Maybe another day, for another child, another family, a miracle will happen. As Kenneth's life ebbed away, Iris said, 'Please God if you have to take him, can my mother look after him? She died young and never had the chance to look after her own children.' I said, 'Take him Father, don't let him linger on.'

And finally it ended. We had reluctantly left the bedside and gone home for a break; the telephone call from the ward sister simply said, 'I'm sorry, Kenneth's dead.'

We returned to the hospital and now, with the tubes and things removed, Kenneth looked quiet, serene, young. We all kissed him and said our goodbyes. Nurses cried in the corner; we knew they had cared even for the short time they had had him. As we came down the stairs from the children's wards for the last time, we wondered how many more children, still there, would die. How many parents would experience this dreadful, tragic, parting? How many would stumble tearfully down these stairs, their beloved child gone, their lives shattered? Perhaps for Billy and the others the miracle would happen. We hoped and prayed that it would.

Now we grieved for our dead son. The sheer physical pain of it, the endless reminders of him – photos everywhere, school books, report cards, football gear, letters that dropped through the letterbox. But we wanted all that around us – he was still part of the family. The weeping, the holding, the talking, the comforting, the grateful presence of our surviving child, Angela – these were the mainstay of our lives.

You learn things very quickly. Are you a crying, weeping family or a silent, withdrawn one? Did you believe that in times of tragedy like this you would be strong and supportive or anguished and distraught? You don't actually have the choice: you are what you are, but you didn't know what that was until now. It may come as a shock in many cases to learn that stereotypes don't always conform. Women are frequently the strong, supportive ones, the men often shattered beyond their capacity to cope.

We talked about Kenneth endlessly, boringly I expect for our friends and relatives who couldn't, in the main, stand it. Their strategy was to change the subject, whereas our strategy was to lead every conversation back to Kenneth. You soon learn that no one really understands, except those who have also lost a child. 'Please, please don't let one other kind person say to me "I understand"', is the commonest outcry from those who have lost a child. Comments such as 'I know how you feel, I lost my granny, my poodle, etc' stretch you to breaking point. I'm sure we said the same kind of things before we lost Kenneth, but even though you know people are just trying to be kind and helpful you are so sensitive and vulnerable that any claim of another person to 'know how you feel' is seen as an attempt to link some suffering of theirs with your shattered existence. The comparisons offered, we know, are simply meant as some bridge by which they can reach us, but sadly the words used create the barrier. Now if they'd put their arms around us, hugged us, kissed us, that would have been different – of course, some of them did.

We were very blessed to have our surviving child, Angela, and later to go on to have another child. Lisa's birth by Caesarean section reminded us how close life and death are at birth. We counted our blessings and said a grateful prayer for our beautiful new child.

Having a new baby, or indeed young children, is not a crutch upon which to hang your grief, but the demand of the infant takes your mind into the practicalities of caring for the precious new life. Lisa also helped fill the great gulf of love left by Kenneth's death.

Then there was Angela, our beloved elder daughter, grieving the loss of her brother and privy to many secrets they shared, which she would tell us in the future. Did she feel pushed out by the never-ending grief of her parents whose every waking moment seemed to extol the virtues of her dead brother? Compared to him, she was entitled to think she was unable to offer us her part-consolation that she was still here, that she was still alive. Thankfully she never rebelled, she just loved and understood us when all the time she was also grieving for a beloved brother.

Perhaps God was helping us in some way just after Kenneth died, but in any event something led Iris to spot the sad obituary for Billy Henderson, the boy who had been in hospital at the same time as Kenneth. He had also died. Iris suggested we send flowers to the funeral. Bill and Joan Henderson telephoned their thanks and asked us round for a cup of tea, that great British institution.

In their company, and they in ours, 'I know how you feel' was very relevant. Of course they knew how we felt, and we them, for hadn't we all just lost a beloved child? Weren't we all experiencing the personal grief that has no equal, no counterpart? In each other's presence, we talked, we cried, we comforted. Unwittingly we had stumbled on the great truth on which The Compassionate

Friends was subsequently founded: 'Bereaved parents can help each other as no one else can as they have experienced the death of a beloved child'. Remember the young clergyman, the Revd Simon Stephens? He was the first to recognise it. He came to see the four of us one evening and said, 'You know, you're helping each other.' And he was right. We helped and comforted each other as no one else could. If that day you'd discovered his exercise book under the bed and you opened it and read 'My Holiday – My Mum and Dad and my sister Angela and me had a smashing holiday in Belgium' or an odd school stocking had surfaced in the wash – the collapsing world about you was not about to be put right by some philosophical prose. What you needed was someone at the end of a phone who would listen to your incoherent outpourings and then tell you they'd be right over. The Hendersons did just that. Perhaps they were having a good day. Maybe tomorrow they'd find the stocking, the exercise book, the football boot and then we would be there for them.

You needed a friend, always available, every day, day or night. That's what Simon Stephens spotted, that's what he meant when he said. 'You know, you're helping each other'. It would be a rather presumptuous thing to say that everything changed there and then for bereaved parents, but it certainly started. When we said we couldn't think why it wouldn't work for other bereaved parents he said, 'Good, I'll call a meeting for next week for all the parents who have lost a child in the last year.'

We had that meeting. Only six people came. But oddly enough the small number didn't seem to deter us; we told our stories anyway and what we talked about most was setting up an organisation to try and help other bereaved parents. It seemed daunting. However, we were fired up with zeal, we wanted to try. What would we call ourselves? The word 'Compassion' had been used more than once during the discussion; it seemed to encompass all that we felt. Suddenly it came to us: 'The Society of The Compassionate Friends'.

It was not an easy start. Bear in mind we – all the founding

Compassionate Friends – were in the first year of our own bereavement. We were incredibly fragile, the events of our children's deaths still as fresh and painful as if it had happened yesterday. But looking at the parents we were visiting, it was clear that we were not grieving quite so much as them – the pain was not as bad as it was for them. This is how we had been six months ago, so perhaps there was a light, however dim, at the end of the tunnel; perhaps they looked at us and were encouraged to live through this dreadful day and live to fight on through the next one, in the hope that one day, however far off, the pain would not be as bad and they could come to peace and a life in which their dead child would have its rightful place.

We soon learned a few hard truths. Trying to get to see bereaved parents was difficult. Often an appropriate condolence or a personal letter was intercepted by a self-appointed censor, who had decided it was 'a family matter' and 'the bereaved parent wants to be left alone in peace'. Soon we decided to wait a couple of weeks and then go round with flowers. Usually we were invited in and then we would be able to talk to them. We would talk about their child, ask what he or she was like and then ask what happened. Usually it would come pouring out, intermingled with tears, sobs, all the pain and suffering.

We were not there to carefully assess another couple's grief, we were not able to give trained and helpful counselling, we just had our grief and they had theirs. We, the Compassionate Friends were there to share our grief, let it intermingle with theirs; to reach out to touch, hug and comfort them and to accept the same support from them when the intensity of our grief itself became apparent to them.

They in truth could help us, it is what I later came to describe as 'The Gift'. Apart from The Compassionate Friends it is the only good thing that came out of the death of our children, if you can ever say that anything good can possibly come out of the death of your child. We did not want it, this 'Gift'. We shouted 'Take it away, turn back the clock, give us back our children.'

But we had it nevertheless, the quite staggering realisation that through the unbearable pain and anguish, you could actually help someone else and they you.

We did not go with instant solutions, with any answers. We were not blessed with the power to take away the pain. We were not clever, we could not rationalise or analyse grief; we simply asked about their child, in a direct way that no one else had done. To let them talk of the sad circumstances of the death, to acknowledge how much they had loved her or him as they cried out their child's name in the pain of it. We had come only with our grief, our despair, our suffering, so that they knew we understood.

We broke every rule of the received wisdom of counselling even then, but that was how it was. We were not counsellors but more importantly perhaps, there was simply an emotional bridge.

We befriended bereaved parents, let them speak, tell their story, let them weep but said one very important thing, 'We will be here for as long as you need us, for as long as you want us.'

It worked, as we always knew it would, for we had asked ourselves, 'What's so different about us?' The answer, 'Nothing, we are the same as everyone else.'

We were not unique, other self-help groups had discovered their own great truths, before and since. We had entered that great taboo field – death and possibly the most sorrowful – the death of children.

Mainly due to the missionary work of Simon Stephens, The Compassionate Friends spread throughout the world, culminating in the First International Gathering in Birmingham in August 1994 to commemorate '25 Caring Years'. It was attended by Compassionate Friends from fourteen countries and was a fitting tribute, certainly 'a memorial to our children' – the phrase coined by our fellow co-founder, the late Bill Henderson.

Iris Lawley was honoured by the MBE in the Queen's 1994

Birthday Honour's list for her work with bereaved parents. There is a certain appropriateness in this for it was her compassionate suggestion, 'Shall we send flowers?' which led to The Compassionate Friends and hopefully support and love for bereaved parents everywhere.

Joe and Iris Lawley
September 1994

HELP AND ADVICE FOR FRIENDS AND RELATIVES OF BEREAVED PARENTS, AND PROFESSIONALS

At the death of a child, parents will need all the help they can get from friends, family and any professionals who are concerned at the time – clergy, doctor, police, social workers, nurses, health visitors.

The following is a brief guideline for those who may be called upon to assist. Every parent is an individual, so it is not meant as a blueprint for helping, nor is it exhaustive.

* Enable the parents to make their own choices and decisions about burial or cremation, choice of service, how to dress their loved ones, how to say 'goodbye', and when and where to dispose of the dead child's possessions. Often this opportunity is thwarted by red tape and conventions and your supporting presence will be invaluable.
* Choose your words carefully and sensitively. We all fall back on clichés in our helplessness, but they often seem cruel and insensitive to parents.
* Share your memories of the child with the bereaved parent, if you knew them before the death. Far from adding to the pain of the parents, they often bring comfort.
* Listen to parents – allow them to talk about their child; the way they died, the way they lived. Help them to relive their memories and to see photographs and relive the good and bad times.

* Do not impose your views and opinions – advice is only helpful when it is requested.
* Physical touch is often important, especially when there are no appropriate words.
* Practical help to parents is useful – cooking, shopping, caring for the other children, even breaking the news to them.
* Let parents know you are thinking of them. Writing a letter to the bereaved parent is so important – you are not imposing.
* Encourage parents in the creative use of grief – writing, painting, gardening, sculpting, even fund-raising for a particular cause, sometimes related to the child's death.
* Make sure that the support structures are in place – family, friends and self-help organisations like TCF, SOS, POMC, etc. (a list follows).
* Allow parents access to as much information as they want. They may need to know the details of what happened to their child, and if they are going to see the body it may help them to know what to expect.

USEFUL ADDRESSES

If you would like more information about The Compassionate Friends contact:

TCF (The Compassionate Friends)
53 North Street
Bristol
BS3 1EN

Tel: 0117 953 9639

* * *

Other bereavement organisations

POMC (Parents of Murdered Children)
c/o John and Irene Baldock
15 Dean Road
Strood
Kent
ME3 3GH

Tel: 01634 718299

SOS (Shadow of Suicide)
c/o Mary Lovegrove
109 Abbeville Road
LONDON
SW4 8JL

Tel: 0171 622 7932

SIBBS (Support in Bereavement for Brothers and Sisters)
c/o The Compassionate Friends
53 North Street
Bristol
BS3 1EN

Tel: 0117 953 9639

SANDS (Stillbirth and Neonatal Death Society)
28 Portland Place
LONDON
W1N 4DE

Tel: 0171 436 7940

CRUSE
126 Sheen Road
Richmond
Surrey
TW9 1UR

Tel: 0181 332 7227

NOTES

(1) Freud, 1913

(2) Translation of a very ancient Chinese poem sent to Countess Mountbatten by an acquaitance in Hong Kong at the time of Nicky's murder. She loved it so much she later had it engraved on his headstone.

(3) Tolstoy, Leo: *Anna Karenina*

(4) Mitchell, Laura: *Simple Relaxation*, John Murray, 1987

(5) Lehmann, Rosamond: *The Swan in the Evening, Fragments of an Inner Life*, Virago, 1982

(6) Gibran, Kahlil: *The Prophet*

(7) Dowd, Michael: *Earth Spirit*